A SHORT HISTORY OF THE PRINTED WORD

HORACE:

The written word remains.

WARREN CHAPPELL

A SHORT HISTORY OF THE PRINTED WORD

NONPAREIL BOOKS · BOSTON

This is a NONPAREIL BOOK published in 1980 by
David R. Godine, Publisher, Inc.
Horticultural Hall
300 Massachusetts Avenue
Boston, Massachusetts 02115

Library of Congress Cataloging in Publication Data

Chappell, Warren, 1904-
    A short history of the printed word.

    Reprint of the ed. published by Knopf, New York.
    Includes index.
    1. Printing—History. I. Title.
[Z124.C47 1980]   686.2'09   79-90409

ISBN 0-87923-312-5

NONPAREIL
BOOKS

Second printing, December 1986

To my friend

ALFRED·A·KNOPF

PREFACE

I N 1922, Harvard University Press published *Printing Types
—Their History, Forms and Use*, by Daniel Berkeley Updike, the outstanding American printer-scholar. The work is
so thoroughly admirable that it has seemed an impertinence for
anyone to offer another history of printing, if only out of
fear of comparison. I acquired my copy of *Printing Types* in
1927, during the time I was working with a New York printer
in order to learn about type and impression firsthand. More
than forty years later, I am struck by the timeliness of Updike's
brilliant presentation, and his conclusion that printing can be

*A broad and humanizing employment which can indeed be
followed merely as a trade, but which if perfected into an art,
or even broadened into a profession, will perpetually open new
horizons to our eyes and opportunities to our hands.*

Updike was not a believer in the good old days. He knew
that it has always been hard to do fine work. The glowing
examples that mark the history of printing do not represent
their periods so much as their dedicated producers, who
managed to perfect their trade into an art. The breadth and
depth and specialization of *Printing Types* make it overpower-
ing for most laymen, and I would venture to say that like Cervantes's *Don Quixote* it is better known by its title than its
text. The possibility that this is true provides a reasonable ex-
cuse for a simpler work, which could serve as an introduction.

In 1927, when I was reading *Printing Types*, I had finished
college, studied at the Art Students League, and had several
years of contact with print-making. By the spring of 1932, I
had added punch-cutting to my experience. Since then I have
had some intimate acquaintance with almost every aspect of
the graphic arts and publishing. I have also been privileged to

know a very large number of the artists, founders, printers, and publishers who have helped to shape the printing of my time.

Now, nearly a half-century after the first edition of *Printing Types*, a bibliophilic friend on the staff of *The New York Times* has insisted that I write a book for laymen about the printed word. The number of visitors to the pressroom of the *Times* and its small typographic museum have convinced him of the need for such a book. It is the mark of a good editor that he can be both persuasive and sustaining.

I hope that my friend is right, and that my very special view of the history of printing is both valuable and communicable. Experience has convinced me that calligraphy and printing have satisfied some of the deepest human needs, intellectually and esthetically. A page of printed type is one of the most abstract pieces of communication I can imagine. Symbols of most ancient origin can be put together in ways that stimulate the eye, through pattern, and the mind, through thought. For this reason, I believe that the area of communication which is now served by printing can never be entirely usurped by any other means.

I think of printing as a medium, and I view the history of printing as a combination of the story of men and materials and the story of the development of the art itself. We are not really concerned here with the greatest, rarest or most beautiful printed works because they are great, rare or beautiful. Rather, our interest lies chiefly in following the most significant developments and influences which have shaped the course of the printed word during the past five centuries. Usually, the examples of printing that are of greatest esthetic merit are also those that have contributed most to the advancement of the craft. Among the influences on printing, illustration has been an important one, because it has generated a continuing search for methods of reproduction, in turn resulting in techniques affecting the manner in which the word was printed. And, after 1814, when the London *Times* used the first power press, newspapers have been an important influence also, since they have played a major role in the development of production tools of the printing industry. It is my belief that both illustration and newspapers deserve important consideration in any history of the printed word.

The strongest feelings I have about printing always return to three simple concepts: the sculptural nature of type, the inevitableness of its arrangement on the page, and the authority of its impression. I offer these to the reader not as a creed but as a working point of view.

ANYONE WHO attempts to recapitulate the essential story of Western calligraphy and printing is aware of his debt to all those who have preceded him, and who made that history or recorded it. In my case, many of those to whom I feel deeply obligated have been my friends for the past four and a half decades. To try to name them all would impose upon the reader.

Instead, I will restrict my list to those who have been intimately involved in making this book, from its conception to production. Initially, it was the request of Allan Ullman, and the strong encouragement of Alfred Knopf, Sidney Jacobs and Oscar Ogg, that made me undertake the task. When the project was originally proposed, Oscar was asked to share it with me, and I regret that he found it necessary, because of other commitments, to withdraw.

In the actual preparation of the manuscript, from typing to copy editing, I have been endlessly aided by Adelaide Sharry, Lee Foster and Judy Pomerantz, and I wish to thank them publicly for their essential contributions. I also want to express my appreciation to Alfred Fairbank for the glimpse of his friend Edward Johnston, which he wrote especially for this volume.

I have thought of this as a book about an art, rather than an art book, and of the illustrations as an integral part of the text.

For this reason, the printing is being done by offset, so that the plates can be shown exactly at the point where they are referred to in the text. The composition, on the other hand, is being done in metal—Linotype for the body matter and captions, and hand-set Monotype for the display half-titles, title page and chapter openings. *The New York Times* assumed the arduous job of locating and photographing most of the two hundred illlustrations that are used. To those who performed that task, and to the museums, libraries, publishers and foundries that cooperated, I am very grateful.

CONTENTS

ILLUSTRATIONS

continued

CHAPTER III

TYPE: CUTTING AND CASTING

CHAPTER IV

THE INCUNABULA: 1400–1500

continued

Illustrations

CHAPTER V

THE SIXTEENTH CENTURY

continued

CHAPTER VI

THE SEVENTEENTH CENTURY

CHAPTER VII

THE EIGHTEENTH CENTURY

continued

CHAPTER VIII

THE NINETEENTH CENTURY

A SHORT HISTORY OF THE
PRINTED WORD

CHAPTER I

Prologue to Discovery

FOR MORE THAN FIVE CENTURIES typographic printing has been a force of incalculable importance. By typographic printing I mean impressions from master alphabets accurately composed into words, lines, and pages. Such printing has been the tool of learning, the preserver of knowledge, and the medium of literature. Until the advent of radio it was *the* great means of communication. The press became and remains a symbol of freedom, defended in Milton's *Areopagitica* and protected in our Bill of Rights.

Yet aside from its communications aspect, printing has had an impressive life as an art and trade. On the lowest level there is a childlike pleasure to be derived from stamping and duplicating which is not greatly removed from making mud pies. On the highest level, that of the best composition and presswork, printing affords the artist the infinitely varied esthetic satisfactions of texture and form.

The key that unlocked practical printing was the devising of movable metal type, cast in molds producing strong and uniform letters and producing them with relatively good speed. From our distance this does not seem like a very large order, technically. However, it is difficult for us to comprehend fully the forces that stood in the way. For instance, paper was not generally available in Europe until the last part of the thirteenth century, documents for the most part being inscribed on parchment or vellum. (Parchment is an animal skin, chiefly that of sheep or goat, which has been scraped, dressed, and prepared for being written on. During the second century B.C., Pergamum became a center for the preparation of skins, and it is from *pergamena* that the word "parchment" is derived. Vellum

[1] Scriptorum.

is parchment made from the skin of a newly born calf, kid, or lamb.) And there were, as always, vested interests which opposed change, especially the organized calligraphers and illuminators, who brought great political pressure to bear to restrict methods of duplication. But the chief deterrent—or, more ac-

A Short History of the Printed Word

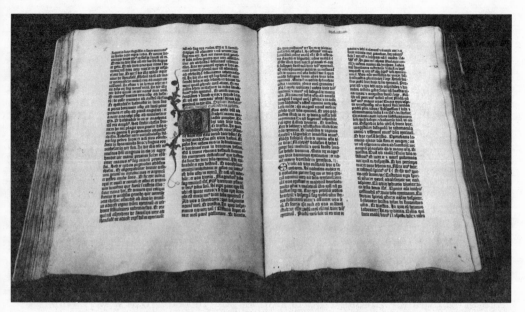

[2] Gutenberg Bible.

curately, the principal reason for apathy—was ignorance. Since so few could read, the need for books was, and continued to be, limited. It required the great surge of the Renaissance to change this.

The Age of Classic Printing

Almost every schoolboy knows that the invention of printing has been credited to Johann Gutenberg even if he does not know that Gutenberg was born Johann Gensfleisch in Mainz circa 1394 and died in 1468. More to the point, it is likely that the average person seeing the excellence of the early books of Gutenberg for the first time would be tempted to doubt that they were the initial manifestations of a new art. Certainly it is common for scholars to assume that there were earlier printed works, especially certain books from a Hollander of Haarlem named Laurens Janszoon Coster, who lived from about 1370 until about 1440. The quality of the early Dutch type-making and printing still extant is so markedly inferior to Gutenberg's that the possibility of a few years' priority is less important than Gutenberg's results. The chief value of establishing earlier experiments lies in their helping to explain the extraordinary quality of the great 42-line Bible—so named because the large majority of the text was set in two columns of 42 lines each—which was printed by Gutenberg between 1452 and 1455.

Since the cutting and casting of the type for this Bible was necessarily preceded by numerous trials to establish means, materials, and techniques, it is safe to say that the invention of printing from movable type dates back to the 1440's, perhaps even the earlier part of that decade. Half a millennium, from then until the mid-1940's with the growth of phototechnology, provides the perfect period for discussing the elements of design, composition, and presswork that constitute the history of printing. By printing I mean the process of transferring images onto paper through the use of types, blocks, plates, or cylin-

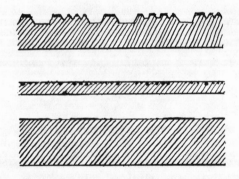

[3] Surfaces: letterpress, intaglio, planographic.

ders. There are three methods, classified as *letterpress, intaglio,* and *planographic* printing. Simply, the first employs a raised image and the second a lowered one. In the case of the third, the principle is one of chemical affinity and the image is level with the surface of the plate or stone. Each method requires a special press, but all three use the term *impression* to describe the pressure that is applied. Thus one speaks of the impression of engraving despite the fact that the image that is lowered in the plate is raised on the paper.

I believe that understanding of the printing medium lies less in dates and personalities than in changing forms and textures.

It is necessary to experience printing by touch as well as sight. For example, a simple tactile response is apparent when a curious layman runs a finger over a calling card or announcement to determine whether the lettering really is *engraved*. A trained eye, figuratively speaking, *feels* impression, and by trained I do not necessarily mean the eye of the professsional designer or printer but that of the dedicated and experienced amateur as well. Goethe said it is necessary to understand the mechanical side of a craft in order to judge it—an opinion at sharp variance with the romantic belief that knowledge and craftsmanship are dangerous and can destroy intuition and sensitivity. To this belief poets have subscribed as well as painters. On the other hand, William Blake, poet *and* painter, and more the man of vision than most, went beyond Goethe. He said that mechanical excellence is the only vehicle of genius. We must keep this in mind in understanding the nature and development of printing.

Using as a neat and workable unit the five hundred years from the mid-1440's to the mid-1940's—the age of classic printing, hot metal, and some form of impression of type on paper—our discussion can range from the invention of cast movable letters to the first large-scale introduction of cameras and film techniques. Coupled with computers, phototechnology is already changing the look and feel of printing as we have known it. Intelligent discussion of the changing directions in contemporary graphic art has to be viewed against the background of past accomplishments, especially of those elements that are the seminal ones, reappearing in every period and every technique. The continuity of printing need not, and should not, be drastically altered by what appears to be a major change of means. Although the new methods may seem to impose fewer restrictions, it is reasonable to assume that the most able artists and craftsmen, regardless of the particular disciplines within which they work, will always hanker after limits to their medium. More than one such artist has contended that it is precisely the limits which bring the master out.

The invention of typographic printing did not drop from

the heavens, although it must have been very much in the air, and the air was becoming increasingly charged, intellectually, by the emerging Renaissance. All of the necessary techniques and materials were there in one form or another. First, it is worth noting that Gutenberg was a goldsmith. His training prepared him for sculpting a letter in steel, from which a casting mold could be made. As long as type-punches were cut by hand, the methods he adapted from his earlier experience changed little in principle, and later techniques seldom contributed any esthetic improvements.

Pre-Typographic Printing

Gutenberg's movable type, like our own, was made in relief. Although impressions from inked raised surfaces had been known in Asia for centuries, this was not true of Europe. Woodcutting is believed to have been practiced in China before the Christian Era, but the earliest dated examples we have are much later, from the ninth century. A very interesting example of Asian wood-block printing is of Japanese origin— the Dharani Scrolls, from the year 770. They were produced at the command of the Empress Shotoku and presented by her to temples throughout her empire, in fulfillment of a religious vow. Originally the thin paper strips were rolled together and housed in a small wooden pagoda-shaped container.

In Europe the technique of printing had to await the introduction and use of paper. As previously indicated, there were also laws, sponsored by scribes and illuminators, which forbade the duplication of images. As a result, the earliest use of wood blocks was for reproducing devotional prints of the figures of saints and the designer-craftsmen were monks working within the privileged walls of their orders. Such woodcuts were being made in the latter part of the fourteenth century, but the earliest dated proofs are from the first quarter of the fifteenth. The St. Christopher (1423) is perhaps the most famous and familiar of these early prints.

The popularity of card-playing helped to stimulate the

[4] Dharani Scroll and container.

early use of block-printing. Since lay wood-block cutters were working outside the law, their cards were printed and distributed in stealth. All means of identification were avoided, thus surrounding the venture with mystery and providing us with a minimum of hard facts about time and origin. It is possible that the Venetian wood-block cutters enjoyed some form of protection by the state, for in 1441 they appealed to the Signoria

Cristofon faciem die quacunq; tueris :·:
illa nempe die morte mala non morieris :·| Millesimo cccc°
                                              x° x° anno :·x·

[5] St. Christopher. Block print dated 1423.

for aid in the form of restrictions on the importation of cards
and printed figures.

The devotional prints were a by-product of pilgrimages
that had been especially encouraged by an increase in the grant-
ing of indulgences for visits to lesser shrines. Before the invention of the press, a common method of taking impressions from
these early blocks was by *frotton printing*—rubbing or bur-

[6] Playing card.

nishing of the back of the sheet, as it rests on the inked block, by means of a suitable tool. In Asia a burnisher for prints still in use is a bamboo leaf stretched over a circular form.

Before the fourteenth century wood blocks had been used in the decoration of textiles. Printed cloth is pre-Christian. Again, however, the earliest known examples are of a much later date. They are Coptic, from the sixth century. In Europe,

Roger of Sicily established a shop for printing cloth at Palermo in the middle of the twelfth century. Examples of cloth and blocks of a century later are in existence. The latter show themselves to be precursors of the blocks that would be made to decorate and illustrate books.

Block-books, on the other hand—that is, books in which a page consisting of picture and words is cut on a single piece of wood—are believed to be of and after the time of Gutenberg rather than before, even though it would be much easier to accept them as forerunners and thus part of typography's pre-natal influence. Their production was obviously due in part to economic considerations, else the practice would not have survived, as it did, into the sixteenth century. Block-books were simple in text, and since their pages existed as independent units, such books could be quickly reprinted on demand without the laborious and costly process of resetting the type.

The bound manuscripts of the fifteenth century were more than mere prefigurements of the first printed books. Rather, they were actual models to be imitated as closely as possible. The purpose of the first printers was to compete with calligraphers. Thus Gutenberg's choice of letter forms was dictated by the popular manuscript hands of the day, not by any inherent characteristics in the methods and materials used for cutting and casting type. Since the alphabet and punch-cutting are the blood and bones of printing, the development of the one and the technique of the other will be given independent treatment in this volume.

The Invention and Spread of Paper-Making

Meanwhile, it has been noted that one of the limiting factors in developing a substitute for manuscript books lay in the lack of a suitable material of which to make them. Vellum was, and is of necessity, a limited and expensive surface. The invention of paper is credited to Ts'ai Lun, a Chinese, in the early years of the second century. (An odd detail to have persisted for so long a time since facts are hard to come by identifies the inventor as a eunuch.) Native fibers—mulberry, bamboo, and others—were soaked and beaten until they became a pulp. The pulp was spread on cloth to form and dry. In time the cloth was replaced by thin bamboo strips, held together by hairs or threads to make a flexible bamboo matting on which the pulp could be drained and formed. The resulting sheet of paper was coarse and long-fibered. This, however, proved no obstacle to the writing instrument it served, which was the brush.

It took a thousand years for Ts'ai Lun's idea to reach Europe. In the interval paper was produced in Japan, early in the seventh century. In the eighth it appeared in Samarkand; the process is thought to have been picked up by Arabs from Chinese prisoners. The Moors may have carried paper-making into Europe. The year 1085 is given as the date of a mill for making paper at Játiva, Spain, that produced a rag sheet, chiefly of linen fibers. The methods of breaking down the fibers, and the materials used for the screen, underwent improvements, and when the first paper mill was established in Italy, at Fabriano, in the latter half of the thirteenth century, stamping machines run by water power had replaced the cruder pounding mortars for producing pulp. In addition, more delicate round wires were substituted for the flat wires of earlier molds. Paper reflected these refinements in terms of weight, flexibility, and fiber character.

After the vatman dipped his mold into the pulp, called *furnish*, he shook or oscillated the frame in such a way that the fibers would be crossed and, thus meshed, would strengthen the sheet. Although the edge of the frame could be made to act as a kind of bench mark, to help determine the amount of pulp to be dipped up, there was great reliance on the experience of the workman. The water having run off, the remaining *water leaf* was *couched*—that is, pressed onto a woolen felt to which it adhered—freeing the mold-screen for reuse. Couched sheets were stacked, pressed, and hung to dry. Finally, they were sized, by being put into a solution of starch or animal glue, to make them less absorbent. Again they were pressed, then hung to dry.

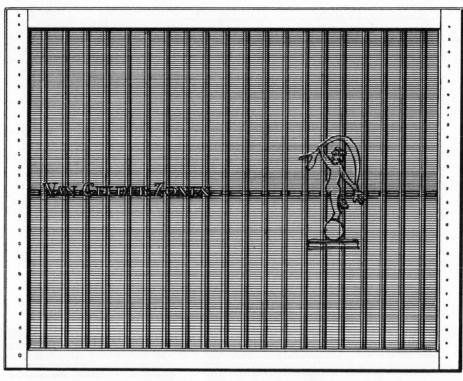

[7] Wire mold for an 18″ × 22″ Dutch-made laid sheet.

Nearly seven hundred years after the setting up of the Fabriano mill, fine handmade paper is still being produced there, in much the same way it was before Gutenberg invented movable type. Once established, paper-making spread rapidly. Among the earliest manufactories were those in France, at Troyes (1338), and in Germany, at Nuremberg (1389). It had taken ten centuries for the concept of turning reconstituted fibers into paper to travel from China to Europe. But between the last years of the thirteenth and the end of the sixteenth century more than sixteen thousand individual watermarks were in use throughout Europe. Watermarks are made from wire formed into simple designs which, in handmade paper, is sewn onto the screen.

Since paper-making at Fabriano began in the late thirteenth century, and the making and dissemination of prints from wood blocks in the fourteenth and early fifteenth centuries, it may be of interest here to list a few names and events which

A Short History of the Printed Word

will give a better sense of the period being discussed. The lives of Dante, Petrarch, Boccaccio, and Chaucer cover approximately a century and a half, from Dante's birth in 1265 to Chaucer's death in 1400. Giotto was born around 1276, Iacopo Bellini around 1400, Masaccio in 1401, and Leonardo da Vinci in 1452, on the very eve of the official birth of printing. Just a year before Leonardo, in 1451, Columbus was born.

In France, the battle of Agincourt took place in 1415, Joan of Arc was burned at the stake in 1431, and the English were finally driven from the country in the middle of the century. It is difficult, at least it is for me, to adjust to the fact that Masac-

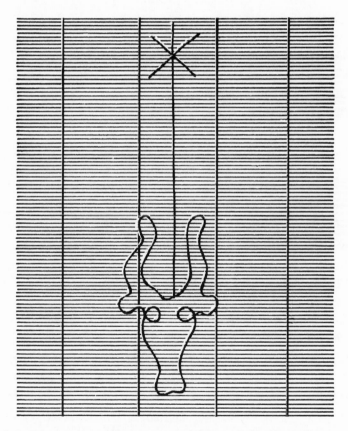

[8] Watermark. The verticals represent the chain lines, and the horizontals the laid lines.

cio's powerful, innovating frescoes in the Brancacci Chapel in Florence were painted, and their creator dead, several years before the execution of Joan of Arc. The first has all the wonder and promise of a new era, the second the dark coloring of the passing Middle Ages.

Humanism and the Renaissance

John Addington Symonds, in his *Renaissance in Italy* (7 volumes, London, 1875–86) writes of three stages in the history of scholarship during the Renaissance:

The first is the age of passionate desire; Petrarch poring over a Homer he could not understand, and Boccaccio in his maturity learning Greek in order that he might drink from the well-head of poetic inspiration, are the heroes of this period. They inspired the Italians with a thirst for antique culture. Next comes the age of the acquisitions and libraries. Nicholas V, who founded the Vatican Library in 1453, Cosimo de Medici, who began the Medicean Collection a little earlier, and Poggio Bracciolini, who ransacked all the cities and convents of Europe for manuscripts, together with the teachers of Greek, who in the first half of the 15th century escaped from Constantinople with precious freights of classic literature, are the heroes of this second period. Then came the third age of scholarship—the age of the critics, philologers, and printers. What had been collected by Poggio and Aurispa had now to be explained by Ficino, Poliziano, and Erasmus. They began their task by digesting and arranging the contents of the libraries. There were no short cuts to learning, no comprehensive lexicons, no dictionaries of antiquities, no carefully prepared thesauri of mythology and history. Each student had to hold in his brain the whole mass of classical erudition. The text and the canon of Homer, Plato, Aristotle, and the tragedians had to be decided. Greek type had to be struck. Florence, Venice, Basel, and Paris groaned with printing presses. The Aldi, the Stephani, and Froben toiled by night and day, employing scores of scholars, men of supreme devotion and of mighty brain, whose work it was to ascertain the right reading of sentences, to accentuate, to punctuate, to commit to the press, and to place beyond the reach of monkish hatred or envious time, that everlasting solace of humanity which exists in the classics. All the subsequent achievements in the field of scholarship sink into insignificance beside the labors of these men, who needed genius, enthusiasm, and the sympathy of Europe for the accomplishment of their titanic task. Virgil was printed in 1470, Homer in 1488, Aristotle in 1498, Plato in 1512. They then became the inalienable heritage of mankind. But what vigils, what anxious expenditure of thought, what agonies of doubt and expectation, were endured by those heroes of humanising scholarship, whom we are apt to think of merely as pedants! Which of us now warms and thrills with emotion at hearing the name of Aldus Manutius, or of Henricus Stephanus, or of Johannes Froben? Yet, this we surely ought to do; for to them we owe in a great measure the freedom of our spirit, our stores of intellectual enjoyment, our command of the past, our certainty of the future of human culture.

This passage from Symonds voices the interest in the Renaissance that was reawakened in England during the latter part of the nineteenth century and culminated in the efforts of William Morris, Emery Walker, and Sydney Cockerell to rediscover and re-employ the techniques of bookmaking as they were practiced in the earliest days of the art. This was essentially a counterrevolt against the Industrial Revolution, which had mechanized printing to a point where its character had been largely sacrificed to expediency. There are few designers of the twentieth century who have not been influenced in some manner or to some degree by the aims and attitudes of that small dedicated group. So it is reasonable to mark the beginning of the final typographic period which closes our prescribed half-millennium of classical printing with the establishment of Morris's Kelmscott Press in 1891 at Hammersmith, London.

If one thinks of industrialism as a new religion—and there

were many who did—then it is possible to relate Morris to the humanists of the fifteenth century who extolled human values and accomplishments and sought to rediscover and preserve them. Theirs was an effort removed from the scholarship of theologians who lost sight of man in trying to rationalize God. The humanism which had been the inspiration of the Renaissance, especially in Italy, came out of the classical culture and cult of antiquity of the fourteenth century. The poet-scholars who did so much to rescue and spread the literature and language of Greece and Rome exerted great influence on their times. They were leaders in cultural and political affairs as well as being the architects of educational methods. In their persons, they were the repositories of the knowledge of antiquity.

One humanist who occupies a special place in the story of printing was the Dutch-born Desiderius Erasmus. He will be met with on several occasions in this history. Here, it is enough to say that among his publications were grammars, dictionaries, a work on Greek and Latin pronunciation, and a book on the art of letter writing. His works had wide circulation. As an example, his *Colloquies*, which appeared in 1516, sold 24,000 copies in a few months.

In addition to the linguistic disciplines developed and strengthened by the study and use of Greek and Latin, the letter forms of our alphabet were preserved for us by the devotion of the humanists to classical culture. The roman capitals we use today are uncorrupted forms of those carved in monuments nearly two thousand years ago.

Bench Marks of Printing

What Morris and his associates began at the Kelmscott Press spread rapidly to Europe and the United States. By the end of World War I, the precious mannerisms and medievalisms of the Pre-Raphaelites and that unfortunate manifestation known as *art nouveau* had been sloughed off, and efforts to recapture basic values in printing craftsmanship became less self-conscious. Central to the attitudes of the fifty years between 1890 and 1940 was a desire to return to original printing surfaces or at least to learn to understand them. That meant of course that artists and printers wanted to circumvent the camera, or control it to a degree sufficient to maintain the integrity of impression and the scale of the original design.

In this second half of the twentieth century, there is an evolving technology in the field of printing that far outstrips in scope and rapidity anything known during the Industrial Revolution. It is necessary more than ever before to measure the new means against their contributions to human values, not to oppose them but to direct them effectively.

What are the bench marks that can serve as references and guides in tracing the history of printing? I would put first an understanding of the alphabet, and an appreciation of its practical as well as its esthetic aspects. Second, a regard for the sculptural nature of type as it was first produced by Gutenberg and perfected by the punch-cutters of the fifteenth and sixteenth centuries. As third and fourth bench marks I would suggest awareness of the arrangement of type and the actual impression from it. These four together determine the form and texture of a piece of printing, and are outside the time flow of people, places, events, developments, and dates. It is possible to put the best piece of contemporary printing beside a page of the Gutenberg Bible, and to compare the two without any concession being asked for the latter because it was produced more than five hundred years ago.

CHAPTER II

The Alphabet

THE LETTER FORMS WE USE stem from lapidary Roman capitals—incised with a chisel—that came to full flower early in the Christian Era. The classic model is the inscription on the column erected in Rome about A.D. 114 by the Emperor Trajan in a Latin alphabet of twenty letters of Greek origin, plus G, Y, and Z. The letters U, W, and J, added to the Latin alphabet centuries after the Trajan capitals, brought the total number up to our present twenty-six characters. U and W are outgrowths of the V form. The letter J, which appeared last, is an alternate form of I.

The symbols that compose our alphabet are phonograms; they are phonetic rather than pictorial; they stand for sounds rather than objects. In fact, they have reached an advanced stage of simplification, where they represent elementary sounds in a progressive change from signs as syllables and, previously, signs as words. Before phonograms, there were ideograms, a more primitive alphabet, with symbols standing for either objects or concepts.

While paleography, the study of ancient writing, is both fascinating and rewarding, too deep a probe into the past here will only confuse. To understand the development of the Latin alphabet up to the invention of type, it is enough to know that the Romans derived their alphabet from the Greeks. They in turn borrowed from the Phoenicians. Letters of the Greek and Phoenician (Semitic) alphabets are closely related in names, forms, and order. For instance, *alpha* and *beta*, the names of the first and second letters in the Greek alphabet, are derived from the Semitic *aleph* and *beth*.

By the ninth century B.C. the Greeks had learned to write.

First, they carried their lines from right to left. Then for a time a method called *Boustrophedon* was used, in which lines were alternated right to left, then left to right. Finally, the line flowed from left to right, as it does today.

Latin manuscripts go back to the first century A.D., and it is

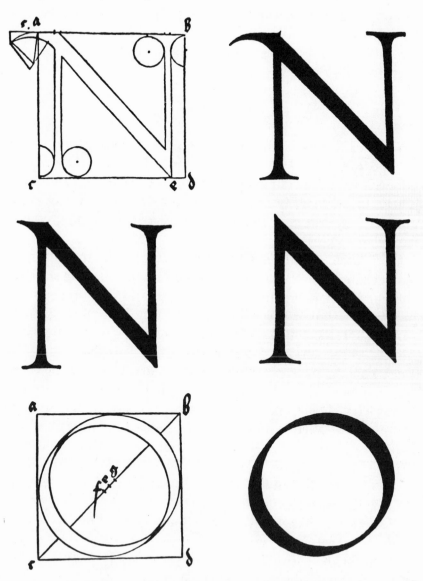

[1] Albrecht Dürer. *Unterweysung der Messung.*

Littera scripta manet

[2] Geofroy Tory. *Bâtarde,* based on his *Champfleury.*

well to understand, from the beginning, that the physical act of writing will play an ever-increasing part in the development of letter forms. The tools used to produce letters have always been formidable forces in developing their character, shape and rhythm.

The Roman Alphabet

Earlier, I stressed my strong belief in the sculptural nature of type. Here, I call attention to the fact that the archetypes for our written and printed alphabets were a set of carved letters. This is echoed, of course, in the original method of type-making, where written forms were translated, sculpturally, into steel.

The great monumental Roman letters can be thought of as having simple geometric bones, so fleshed-out that the straights and curves relate organically. A letter should seem to be of one piece, not a sum of parts. The round forms bespeak circles and parts of circles. But despite many efforts to develop formulae for the construction of the alphabet, such as those made by Luca Pacioli, Albrecht Dürer, and Geofroy Tory, no set of rules can be slavishly held to. The subtleties of the great Roman forms have always eluded the compass and square. The perfect expression of a letter remains in the mind of an artist as a pure concept of form, essentially abstract in nature. Just as a draftsman uses a model for a figure drawing, a letter artist should respond through memory and the particular tool in his hand to the special requirements of his design.

There are several ways of reaching a general understanding of the basic nature of roman. One logical and rewarding way is to think of the forms as a series of geometrical variations on a theme of square, circle, and triangle, which, when set together,

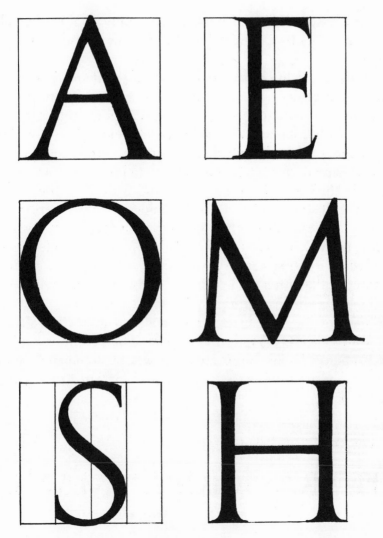

[3] Trajan capitals set against square fields to demonstrate
the proportions and rhythms of roman.

will become a frieze of contracting and expanding spatial inter-
ruptions. This breathing quality is the very essence of the inscriptional concept, and is responsible for the liveliness as well
as the nobility of the great classic carvings. Almost every letter
shape carries its contained space, which in type is called the
counter, and which is related, in composition, to the separations

between letters. This inner space is not only vital to the color of a form—its black-and-white value—but is also an integral part of it.

If, in visualizing roman, one thinks of the shapes in relationship to square fields, proportion can be more dramatically understood in a structural way, and the variations from narrow S to wide M become clear as skeletal archetypes. This is perhaps better shown than described. Here, several letters based on the Trajan capitals are set against square fields, which are subdivided in the cases of the narrow E and S to show their forms against half the field. The thick-and-thin characteristics of these examples indicate their development from written forms produced with a wide-edged tool. In Pompeii, which was destroyed in the first century A.D., there are examples of mural writing made with a flat brush. This would be an obvious way of laying in an inscription to be incised in stone. Thus the antiquity of the flat-edged instrument is established in shaping the appearance of Western alphabets. The centuries between the Emperor Trajan and Gutenberg will be dominated by calligraphy, written with reeds and quills sharpened to a wedge-shaped point.

Ameliorations of Roman

LITTERA SCRIPTA MANET

[4] Square capitals.

The more formal written alphabet of this early Roman period was known as square capitals (*capitalis quadrata*). These capitals were used for important works from the second century into about the fifth century, and their proportions had much in common with the lapidary capitals. The principal differences lay in their strong contrasts of thicks and thins, and the pen-derived serifs of the square capitals. A serif is a terminal device, functionally employed to strengthen lines which otherwise would tend to fall away optically. This is especially true

[5] Square capitals.

of incised lines. By using a chisel in such a way that the finishing cuts were wider, a craftsman produced a strong terminal with a bracketed appearance. Performing a similar function for type, serifs continue to be seen on the majority of faces in general use. They derive more often from the example of the chisel than of the pen.

Square capitals are not easy to write, and this limited their wide usage. The story of writing can be told in terms of the search for simpler forms, requiring fewer strokes and pen lifts and providing their own beat or rhythm to such an extent that spacing for color and legibility could be more easily controlled.

Such an amelioration is expressed in the rustic capitals (*capitalis rustica*) of the same period, roughly, as the square capitals. These rustic letters anticipate an ever-recurring tendency to condense, usually to save space. Such economy was indicated when the material to write on was rare and costly vellum. By holding a flat-nibbed pen or wedge-shaped brush at an acute angle, the writer thins the verticals to a point where they become little more than a recurring beat, against which the

[6] Rustic capitals.

[7] Rustic capitals.

round and diagonal strokes make their pattern and the horizontals provide their accent. Much could be learned from these early forms that would be of value in designing a condensed type face for use in newspaper headlines. Forms essentially full and round cannot be accommodated to narrow usage simply by squeezing them together. The color-clotting in the joints of many headline faces could be avoided by designs stemming from naturally condensed forms.

By the fourth century, there developed a style of writing that had as its chief characteristic the rounding off of certain angles and joints. This style, called *uncials*, carried into the eighth century. Rounded forms were used chiefly to increase speed, since the curves reduced the number of strokes necessary to shape the letters. They flow directly and easily from a quill or reed, and therefore have a natural authority, in addition to aiding legibility. The style affected the forms of A, D, E, H,

[8] Uncials.

M, U, and Q. As noted, earlier angular pen-written joints are hard to keep clear and open. Since they are prone to filling up and darkening in color, they can be spotty in the mass.

26

[9] Uncials.

Up to this point, Roman letters have stood between two hypothetical horizontal lines. Early in the sixth century, the *half-uncial*, or *semi-uncial*, came into use. This marked a change to a true variant on capitals, and was the beginning of what we think of as lower case. Instead of two lines enclosing the forms, four lines are implied in the half-uncials; ascending and descending elements were introduced. This new variation provided an alphabet that was easier to write and could have great intrinsic beauty as well—witness the Irish and English versions of the half-uncial. A notable change in the curves of

[10] Semi-uncials.

[11] Semi-uncials.

these alphabets was caused by the manner in which the pen was held, horizontal to the line, as opposed to the strongly slanted position used for writing rustic capitals. Half-uncials belong to the seventh, eighth, and ninth centuries.

On the Continent, the calligraphic hands of this general period had degenerated, especially in comparison to the work being done in England and Ireland. Under the influence of a corrupted Roman cursive, best described as a running script, Europe's book hands had suffered. There had been no unifying force to fill the vacuum caused by the dissolution of the Roman Empire, and it was only natural that all means of expression fell victim to provincialism.

The Caroline Minuscule

Such was the state of calligraphy when Charlemagne came to power in 768. By decree, in the year 789, he ordered a revision of the books of the Church. His plans do not seem to have envisioned textual revision; instead, he wanted the most

[12] The Caroline minuscules.

28

[13] The Caroline minuscules.

beautiful and accurate copies made of the finest existing manuscripts. Success for such an undertaking called for the development of a standard model hand that could be practiced throughout the Emperor's domains. The result was the beautiful
Caroline minuscule, a true small letter, with definite classic
ancestry, but employing a four-line system. Credit for the alphabet is given to Alcuin of York, Abbot of St. Martin's,
Tours, from 796 to 804.

The spread of this letter was rapid, not only in France but
in all of western Europe, where it was dominant for many
years. Introduced into England in the tenth century, it was
generally adopted there after the Norman Conquest. The Caroline minuscule is the true ancestor of our lower-case printing
type. The forms are simple, clear, and handsome, rounded and
relatively wide. The alphabet tends to avoid cursive forms and
excessive ligatures, especially those that would change its character, and it keeps the letters independent of one another. Those
curved forms that spring from straight stems have an organic

relation to the source, much as a growing leaf does in nature. All of these considerations have a strong bearing on the making of a workable, movable cast type for printing.

In addition to looking like lower case, the Caroline minuscule was used in the same way. Majuscules, or capitals (often built up with more than a single pen stroke), started a sentence that continued in minuscules. Improvement in the organization of the text, through better punctuation as well as sentence and paragraph arrangements, is also credited to this thoroughly constructive period. The flourishing centuries of manuscript production during the Caroline influence did much more than establish a fresh start on a common writing hand. It is generally conceded that without the appearance of the Caroline reform, coupled with the scholarly enterprise of the period, there would have been serious losses in the quality of the texts which reached the Renaissance. In most instances, it appears, the preferred texts were those preserved in manuscripts of the ninth and tenth centuries.

Despite the wide appeal and use of the Caroline minuscule, its uniformity and high standards could not be maintained. Inevitably, national characteristics and experience were impressed upon the original models to such an extent that numerous hands resulted. The large divisions were essentially geographical, that is, north and south. Thus the writing in France, the Low Countries, and England showed some kinship, at least for a time, and Italy, Spain, and southern France shared certain common characteristics of style.

Post-Caroline Hands

By the eleventh century, there was a general tendency toward smaller and more condensed letters. Again, this was certainly due, in part, to a desire to economize on parchment as well as on time. However, compression of forms for style's sake is one thing; quite another is the development of a more measured system of spacing by using an alphabet of greater homogeneity. The calligrapher managed, in first reducing the full

Littera scripta manet

[14] *Textur* of Gutenberg's time.

round forms and then finally eliminating them, to acquire a completely different rhythm. Roman capitals have been described as having a breathing rhythm; the gothic lower case has the pattern of a picket fence. To some degree, the achievement of even color throughout the page was partly mechanical, due to the regular beat of the verticals and the evenness of the counters. The diagonal couplings and footings of the letters gave them a pointed effect, but they also served as terminal accents, similar in function to serifs. This so-called gothic script underwent numerous transitional forms. It was known in fourteenth-century Germany as *Textur*, in France as *lettre de forme*, and in England as *black letter*. It was a *lettre de forme* of the following century that served as a model for the type used in Gutenberg's 42-line Bible and in the Mainz Psalter.

Southward, in Italy and Spain, there was strong resistance to the harsh, acute angles of northern contemporaries. There, a

[15] Black letter. Fourteenth-century breviary.

Littera scripta manet

[16] *Rotunda* based on Cresci models.

rounder "gothic," called *Rotunda*, was developed. It was as rich in color as the black letter, but its style was reminiscent of a classic roman heritage, especially as expressed in the Caroline minuscule. In general, the "gothic" scripts are considered to be variations on the Caroline even when the modifications seem extreme.

Humanistic Script and Chancery Cursive

Rotunda was not the only attempt to resist the northern gothic style. There was also the neo-Caroline letter, a Renaissance roman hand, known as *scrittura umanistica*, which most directly relates our present lower-case type to the earlier Caroline minuscule. In the fifteenth century, the Renaissance had

EƐƐƐeee

[17] The development of written hands from the time of the square capitals to the *scrittura umanistica*.

rekindled enthusiasm for classic culture and calligraphers sought pre-gothic models for their transcriptions of classical texts. The result of their efforts was not merely a resurrection of ninth-century writing. For their new, written capitals they used the early lapidary letters as models.

The humanistic script was a more compressed letter than its Caroline predecessor, but it was significantly rounder than the northern gothics it was destined to supplant. Early manuscripts

littera ſcripta manet

[18] *Scrittura umanistica.*

in this script (late fourteenth, early fifteenth centuries) tended to be labored and unsteady. The period when the first great examples of printing were being produced witnessed the perfecting of the hand.

From the standpoint of the scribe, the gothics had many advantages, especially in ease of writing. In addition, there is the essential authority of black letter that derives from its being a lower-case alphabet, devised to solve basic writing problems.

Inuentarium Argenteorum & paramentor
donata sunt per Ill.m et Ex.m Ludouicu M
sfortiam Anglum Mli ducem: ecclie sce M
gratiar in suburbijs porte vercelline m
Pro Altari maiori
Primo. Crux una magna argentea cum pede
instar unius montis in quo sunt tres figure
beate uirginis Marie. sce marie magdalen
sci iohannis eglište. super crucem autem so
cum quadam capseta in pede pro conden
liquijs. Ponderis o3 Vxx
Item tabernaculum unū argenteum desup
tum pro corpore xpi deferendo. in quo sun
figure. V3. sci Dominici. et sci petri marti
in summitate eius figura xpi resurgentis
o3 clxVii

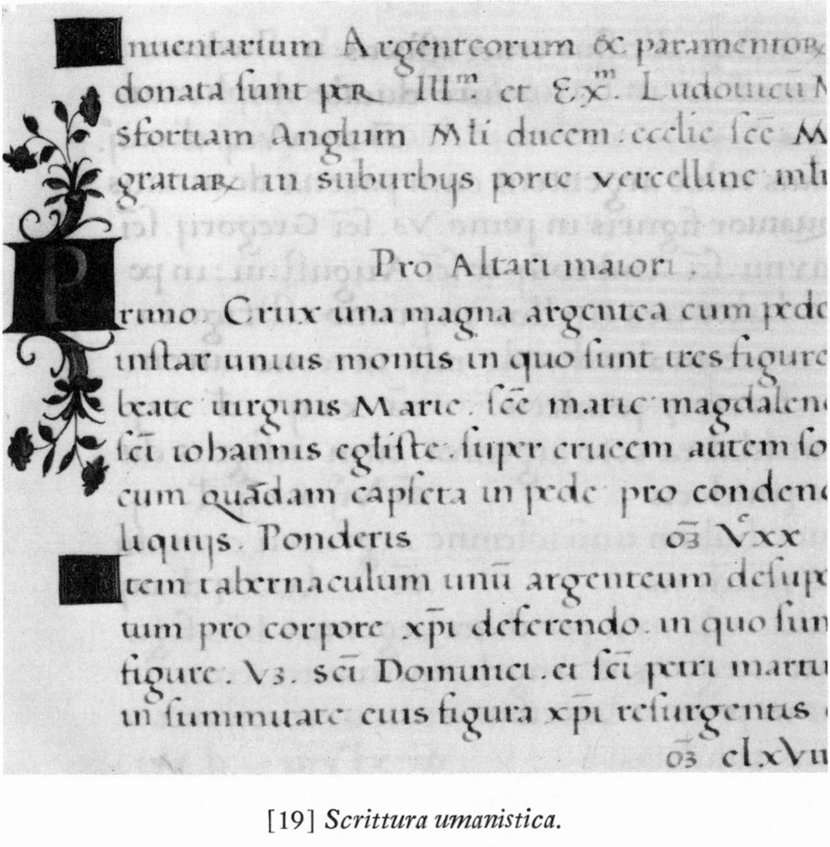

[19] *Scrittura umanistica.*

This cannot be said of the majuscules developed to fit with the gothics.

With roman the situation is reversed: the capitals have the authority and the lower case is a series of improvisations. The elegance achieved by the use of long ascenders and descenders can so reduce the middle, or x, height of roman lower case that the type face appears small. This is especially noticed where space limitations require a high letter count to the line. Despite all calligraphic shortcomings, however, the eventual precedence of roman must have played a significant and happy part in preventing the re-emergence of numerous and confusing national hands.

Fairly early in the history of printing, *cancellaresca*, an offspring of the *scrittura umanistica*, was translated into types, the first italic. Although first used chiefly to save space, in time it became the basic typographic tool for accent.

Of all the semi-formal hands developed over the years of the emerging Latin alphabet, *cancellaresca*, or chancery script (so-called because of its use by papal secretaries), is unquestionably the most beautiful. It has some general interest today because of the efforts that have been made, especially in the last half century, to revive it for correspondence.

Chancery cursive was an outgrowth of the neo-Caroline hand, written with greater speed. The tendency was toward a slope, but slanting was not obligatory. The cursive quality was built into the letters. First, the forms were more compressed than *scrittura umanistica*, and, as in the case of black letter, the rhythmic beat of nearly even strokes and spaces created a characteristic pattern. Round forms became elliptical, approaching a parallelogram. Roman capitals were used, but they were small in relationship to the over-all height of the four-line system.

[20] *Cancellaresca*. Chancery script.

Littera scripta manet

[21] Chancery script, early sixteenth century.

The Final Flowering of Calligraphy

This chapter began with the statement that today's letter forms stem from the great Roman capitals of more than eighteen centuries ago. With the perfecting of the humanistic script in the fifteenth century, the esthetics of type design had come full circle and classic forms were again firmly established as ideal archetypes. Finally, the various expressions of the alphabet could be divided into three classes: formal, semi-formal, and epistolary, which, rendered into the type faces we know, are recognized as capitals, lower case, and italic.

In many places, notably Florence, the coming of printing was strongly resisted. Scribes understandably set themselves against such an economic threat and their patrons were often equally contemptuous of what they considered the crude and vulgar imitations of good manuscripts.

In *The Civilization of the Renaissance in Italy*, Jakob Burckhardt gives an interesting picture of the libraries and the copyists at the time of the *incunabula*, those first printed books:

The library of Urbino, now in the Vatican, was wholly the work of the great Frederick of Montefiltro. As a boy he had begun to collect; in after years he kept thirty or forty scrittori employed in various places, and spent in the course of time no less than 30,000 ducats on the collection. It was systematically extended and completed, chiefly by the help of Vespasiano, and his account of it forms an ideal picture of a library of the Renaissance. At Urbino there were catalogues of the libraries of the Vatican, of St. Mark at Florence, of the Visconti at Pavia, and even of the library at Oxford. It was noted with pride that in richness and completeness none could rival Ur-

35

bino. Theology and the Middle Ages were perhaps most fully represented. There was a complete Thomas Aquinas, a complete Albertus Magnus, a complete Bonaventura. The collection, however, was a many-sided one, and included every work in medicine which was then to be had. Among the 'moderns' the great writers of the 14th century, Dante and Boccaccio, with their complete works occupied first place. Then followed twenty-five select humanists, invariably with both their Latin and Italian writings, and with all their translations. Among the Greek manuscripts the fathers of the church far outnumbered the rest; yet in the list of classics we find all the works of Sophocles, all of Pindar, all of Menander. The last must have quickly disappeared from Urbino, else the philologist would have soon edited it.

We have, further, a good deal of information as to the way in which manuscripts and libraries were multiplied. The purchase of an ancient manuscript, which contained a rare, or the only complete, or the only existing text of an old writer, was naturally a lucky accident of which we need take no further account. Among the professional copyists, those who understood Greek took the highest place, and it was they especially who bore the name of 'scrittori.' Their number was always limited, and the pay they received very large. The rest, simply called 'copisti,' were partly mere clerks who made their living by such works, partly school masters and needy men of learning, who desired an addition to their incomes. The copyists at Rome in the time of Nicholas V were mostly Germans and Frenchmen—'barbarians,' as the Italian humanists called them, probably men who were in search of favors at the papal court, and who kept themselves alive meanwhile by this means. When Cosimo de' Medici was in a hurry to form a library for his favorite foundation, the Bardia below Fiesole, he sent for Vespasiano, and received from him the advice to give up all thoughts of purchasing books, since those that were worth getting could not be had easily, but rather to make use of the copyists; whereupon Cosimo bargained to pay him so much a

*day, and Vespasiano, with fifty-five writers under him, deliv-
ered 200 volumes in twenty-two months.*

*The material used to write on when the work was by great
or wealthy people was always parchment; the binding, both in
the Vatican and at Urbino, was a uniform crimson velvet with
silver clasps. Where there was so much care to show honor to
the contents of a book by the beauty of its outward form, it is
intelligible that the sudden appearance of printed books was
greeted at first with anything but favor. Frederick of Urbino
'would have been ashamed to own a printed book.'*

CHAPTER III

Type: Cutting and Casting

W HEN GUTENBERG began searching for a practical way to make movable type, he had no question about the character of the letter he was looking for: the best possible imitation of the most highly regarded manuscript hand of his day. Fortuitously, the northern gothics were at that time in the ascendency in Mainz. It is likely that this accident helped the first type-cutter, because just as gothic letter forms are easier to write than roman, they are also easier to cut. There is less subtlety in gothic shapes as well as in the mechanics of joining them in words and sentences.

For the purpose of describing the manner in which type-punches are cut by hand, I prefer to use roman letters as examples. Within fifteen years of Gutenberg's initial achievement, several romans of lasting value and wide influence had appeared. In time, of course, roman superseded gothic everywhere except in Germany. There, *Frakturs*, *Schwabachers*, and some *Rotundas* continued to enjoy fairly wide use until World War II, when they were supplanted by roman fonts.

Tools and Preparation

At the heart of learning to produce movable type was the invention of a suitable mold for casting. Some of the earliest trials employed sand or clay, but such a primitive approach was impractical as well as esthetically unsatisfying. The solution was a metal mold, which would accommodate individual metal matrices. To produce such matrices, punches were required. The skills needed to cut and use punches were a part of the goldsmith's apprenticeship; one of his first exercises was to

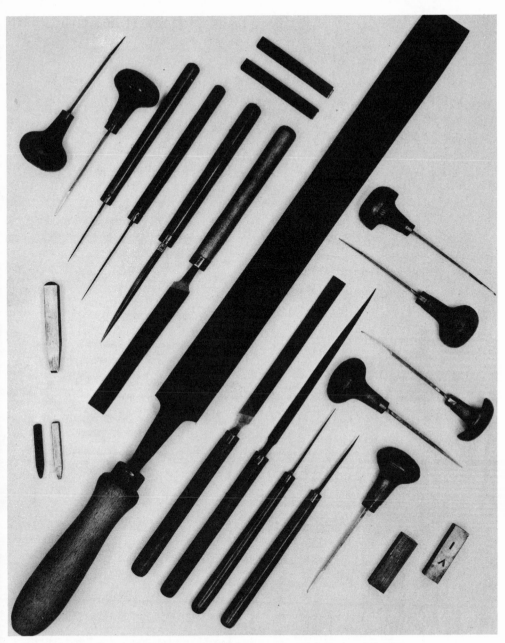

[1] The author's files and gravers. Photographed by Philip
Van Doren Stern in 1932.

make his chasing tools, which *are* punches.

The stock for a punch is square rod of carbon steel, averaging two and a quarter inches in length and having a face of

CHAPTER III • *Type: Cutting and Casting*   39 sufficient size to contain the letter. Besides gauges and squares, the tools required by the punch-cutter are numerous files and gravers, and a special instrument or two. Files are of three kinds: big, fast-cutting files used in the preliminary dressing and shaping of the punch; medium-size files, fine-textured for the most part; and small-size ones that take a minimum bite from the steel. The gravers used in type-cutting are straight-

[2] A type-cutter's graver.

bellied; they do not have the sweeping keel of those used by wood engravers. From the beginning and for centuries afterward, the type-cutter also needed counter-punches, square steel rods, smaller than the punches, on the end of which were fashioned shapes that when hardened were struck into the punch itself. The depression was thus formed, comparable to

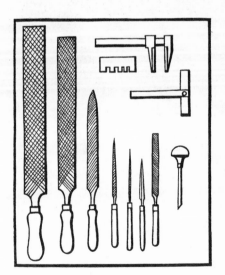
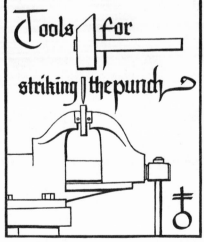

[3] Diagram by Rudolf Koch showing the simple tools and gravers of a punch-cutter.

[4] Rudolf Koch filing a punch against the pin. In the fore-
ground are heavier files, gravers, and a stake for
counter-punching. At the rear can be seen a vise, a
torch for hardening the finished punches, and stones on
which the surfaces are planed.

the space within a letter, called the counter. The letter-shape
was then filed around the depression in the punch, giving maximum clarity to the inner white space of each letter.

The first task of the type-cutter is to prepare the steel stock.
The bars are planed with a heavy file so that two sides are
finished, smooth, and at right angles. Then, on each, a terminal
is so fashioned that the force of the strike will be delivered
through the center of the punch. The face end of the punch is
finished, first filed at right angles to the finished sides, then
polished. In each bar, near the butt end, a mark is filed to

Singe den Groll, o Göttin, des Peleussohnes Achilleus,
Der, ein Verderber, erschuf unendliche Not den Achäern,
Und viel tapfere Seelen gewaltiger Streiter zum Hades
Sendete.
I=\/O°ABCDEFGHIJKLMNOPQR
STUVWXYZ · ✁ ✁ + + + + + +
a · b · c · d · e · f · g · h · i · j · k · l · m · n · o · p · q ·
r · s · t · u · v · w · x · y · z + ß ß +

Singe den Groll, o Göttin, des Peleussohnes Achilleus
Der, ein Verderber, erschuf unendliche Not, den Achäern,
Und viel tapfere Seelen gewaltiger Streiter zum Hades
Sendete.
O°ABCDEFGHIJKLMNOPQR
STUVWXYZ
abcdefghijklmnopqrstuvwxyzßß

[5] Calligraphy and completed type. Koch *Antiqua*, produced by Klingspor.

indicate the bottom of the letter-to-be; this corresponds to the nick in type, and serves the same purpose.

Among the basic pieces of equipment needed is a *pin*, similar to that used by a goldsmith or jeweler. It is a projection of wood, nicked to allow the work to be held and backed-up for filing and engraving. The punch-cutter's version of this simple adjunct of his bench is placed at about chest height. There must also be a vise available to hold the punches for fast shaping with the heavy file. A two-power magnifying glass, or loop, and a proper stand to hold it are required. A fourth basic necessity is a planer, in which the punch can be held for resurfacing its

A Short History of the Printed Word

face. Such resurfacing can be done with a hard stone, such as one used for sharpening tools, or with an abrasive sprinkled on a flat area. The device that keeps the punch at right angles to the planing surface is merely a block of steel with a corner angle machined into it.

The Counter-Punch

Punches for the first printing types were not cut from specially designed alphabets. Since Gutenberg and many of his followers were chiefly interested in trying to imitate existing manuscripts, it is reasonable to assume that the models were chosen directly from such manuscripts and translated into steel. These early type faces were the same size as their calligraphic originals and many stylistic idiosyncrasies were apparent in both type and model. When I worked with Rudolf Koch, it was extremely interesting to me to observe that he still used the calligraphic approach for a number of his types. He wrote long passages, then went through them underlining the letters he regarded as most successful. His Koch *Antiqua* is shown here in calligraphy and as type.

As an example of counter-punching techniques, a roman capital H is chosen to take through the process. This allows me to use a set of illustrations which were made by Professor Koch in 1932. Here the inner space is divided into two parts by the

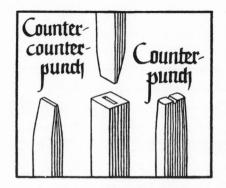

[6] Diagrams of counter-punching by Rudolf Koch.

crossbar; it is more than a simple rectangle with round corners. To achieve the crossbar, the counter-punch must then be so shaped that a trench made in it will allow the crossbar to remain standing after the punch is struck. Such a trench could be shaped by filing. An accomplished punch-cutter, however, would prefer to use a wedge-shaped counter-counter-punch to provide the trench. Thus, in this case the counter-punch starts out looking like a rectangle with a depression

[7] Counter-punching stake.

across it. The surface of the second punch is disturbed by the strike and has to be replaned. The first, rough-shaping file cuts are made in a vise. Then the counter-punch can be worked against the pin and given its form. The face of a counter-punch shapes the floor of the final counter. It is the rim, at a depth equal to the strike, which determines the inner margin of the letter. To test progress, the counter-punch is struck, after each revision, into a piece of lead. Such a lead surface may be hammered out, after it has been filled with strikes, and used again.

When a counter-punch has been brought to its final form, it must be hardened before it is used for striking. First it is heated to a cherry red and chilled. In that stage the steel is glass-hard and brittle. It must be annealed by reheating it to a straw color in order to keep it from cracking under stress.

To strike the counter into the face of the punch stock, it is best to have some sort of *stake* to hold the two steel rods steady in their related positions. The simplest stakes are merely adjustable collars, while a more advanced version has its own heavy base to provide extra draw under the force of the hammer. When the strike into the punch is made, metal is displaced and the face of the punch is distorted, just as it was when the counter-punch was made. The bar of steel must be put in the planing angle and its surface refinished. The diagram indicates

[7a] Planer.

the face of a punch at this stage: flat, with a two-part rectangular depression. The letter as cut and as cast is reversed, i.e., the mirror image of the printed impression. The punch is now put into the vise and roughed down to its H form, initial shaping being made at a relatively obtuse angle. Afterwards, the type bar is worked against the pin with flat, round, and triangular files. Perhaps the most useful of the file shapes is the double half-round (*bird's tongue*). It is better than a flat file for achieving a straight stem, because a flat file tends to bite faster at the terminals of a line.

If the punch-cutter has been lucky, the inner form of the letter was completed with the striking of the counter-punch. At any point in the process, a proof of the work is easily taken by bringing the punch up close to the flame of an alcohol lamp. This causes the face of the punch to sweat, and when plunged into the flame, its tip acquires a coating of lampblack. When touched to a piece of chalky cameo paper, the punch leaves a brilliant image.

The Sculptural Aspect

At this point it is easy to understand the value of the careful preparation of the steel stock. Since two sides are squared to each other and to the face of the punch, and since these relationships have in turn been adjusted to the angle of the planer during the final grinding of the face, it is possible to change this angle by filing the sides of the punch. The resulting change of cant makes possible swift renewal of the surface of the metal by planing any selected part of the face. Thus correcting can be carried on without extensive recutting. It is an essential virtue of the punch-cutting method that the design is constantly in flux. The weight of an entire alphabet may be changed simply by putting it on the planer.

Although Gutenberg was interested in imitating the appearance of manuscript books, his means of producing an alphabet did not imitate calligraphic practice. His written models were translated into steel through a sculptural process. All the refinements were carried forward by direct and plastic means. Even in the use of engraving tools, type-cutting calls for handling that is much more related to scraping and paring than to delineating. As it was practiced in the earliest days of printing, punch-cutting, coupled with the high state of calligraphy during the fifteenth and sixteenth centuries, produced a series of faces which are still the major models for many of the types we use today.

Once the smoke-proofs show that the desired form has been achieved, the angle of the punch, from face to sides, is made steeper. For purposes of correction an obtuse angle was needed; for striking, a steeper one is obviously more practical. Finally, the punches are hardened and annealed.

Chapter III · *Type: Cutting and Casting*

Striking and Justifying the Matrix

Accuracy and strength were the characteristics which Gutenberg sought in developing movable type casting. Accuracy was not just a matter of the height of the type. It was also necessary that every dimension be as compatible as possible and that the position on the body be constant so that dancing lines are avoided. To cast type consistently, a matrix had to be developed along with an adjustable hand mold that would carry it. The chief ingredient of type metal was lead, to which antimony was added for hardening and tin for its melting properties. In addition to durability, casting quality had to be considered in choosing the components of the metal. For the matrix, a material which would properly respond to the strike was needed. Copper had many advantages and was preferred to brass, which, although longer-lived than copper, was harder on

[8] Original Janson mats, photographed for the author by D. Stempel, the present owners (*enlarged*).

the punches. When the letter has been depressed into the surface of the matrix, any metal which has been upset must be planed down. This planing is done with a file laid flat. The matrix, held with the fingers of both hands, is worked across the file. A needle depth gauge is used to test the floor of the strike in relation to the face of the matrix. The leveling and squaring-up of the strike, by alternate filing and testing, is known as *justification*.

Hand Casting

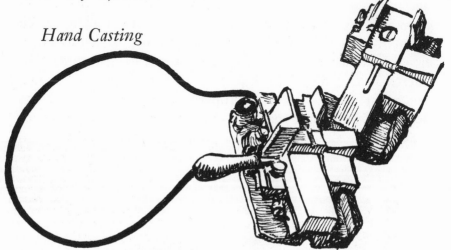

[9] Hand-casting mold, showing inner construction.

The casting of type was Gutenberg's great contribution to practical printing. The art changed little for several centuries. There were improvements in the composition of type metal and in the design and construction of the hand mold, but the basic techniques were not greatly altered.

The mold shown here incorporates some improvements on the first model, but it is still simple in construction and in use. It consists of two halves that fit together to form a casting box of adjustable dimensions. When the matrix is put in place in this mold, it blocks one end. The matrix is held by the strong horseshoe-shaped spring. The other end of the mold is flared so that it forms a funnel shape when the two halves are put together. This device aids the drop of the type metal into the

[10] Hand-casting mold, gauges. Bottom center, needle
depth-gauge described under *justifying*. Photographed
by Philip Van Doren Stern in 1932.

mold. The flared shape, known as the *jet*, was not present in the
first molds.

The mold allows numerous adjustments to position the letter on the body and to control the body width. As a protection
for the type-caster, the two halves are encased in wood. The

wood covers can be replaced if they become broken or badly burned out. Hot metal is dipped from a crucible with a small ladle. As it is poured into the mouth of the mold, a jerk of the instrument or a blow against the spring, often by raising the thigh, gives extra thrust to the metal for sharper castings.

After casting, the jets are broken off. The type is put in a *dressing stick* and finished with a planelike tool. This assures that the letter is type-high (0.918 inch), and it cuts the basal groove as well as smoothing the feet. The finished product is composed of numerous parts, more easily named and understood in this diagram reproduced from the drawing made by Rudolph Ruzicka for D. B. Updike's *Printing Types—Their History, Forms and Use.*

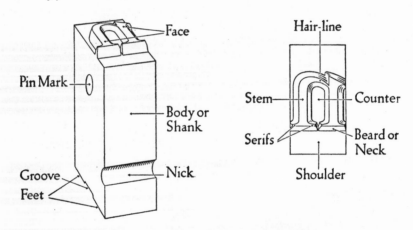

[11] Plan and nomenclature of a piece of type.

In the early years, printers cast their own types. There were no uniform standards and some printers favored nonconforming typographic material to discourage pirating of their designs. The sixteenth century saw the establishment of independent type foundries, and as these increased in number there were demands for more uniformity. But there were many problems, and solutions to them were few and slow in coming, and not always happy ones. The American point system finally gave some order to typographic measurements, but it was not generally adopted in this country until the 1870's.

CHAPTER III · *Type: Cutting and Casting*

The idea of a point system originated in 1737 with Pierre Fournier, a French type founder. In the present system, there are approximately 72 points to the inch (a point is 0.0138 inch) with 12 points making one pica. Before the adoption of the American point system, type sizes were indicated by names, such as nonpareil, brevier, and pica, etc. With the point system, those sizes became 6-point, 8-point, and 12-point.

The Font

A font (or fount) of type is the complete collection of its characters in a given size. As an example, the text of this book is set in 12-point Linotype Janson, a roman design that appeared in America in 1934. It is derived from a set of seventeenth-century punches in the possession of the Stempel foundry of Frankfurt that were believed to be the work of Anton Janson, who was trained in Amsterdam by Christoffel van Dijck and worked in Frankfurt and Leipzig about the middle of the seventeenth century. More recently, the punches have been thought to be the work of a Nicholas Kis, a Hungarian who may have learned his trade from the Dutch type founder Dirk Voskens.

ABCDEFGHIJKLMNOPQRSTUVWXYZ
ABCDEFGHIJKLMNOPQRSTUVWXYZ
abcdefghijklmnopqrstuvwxyz
Æ Œ æ œ æ œ fi fl ff ffi ffl
AÁÄ EÉ Ií
ÁÀÂ Ä Ç ÉÈÊË Í Ö Ü
áàâäăãąåâ çć éèêëēĕėê îìîïī ńñ óòôöōŏô
ōō ŏŏ śş úùûüūŭů
1234567890   1234567890
£ $ ℔ @ & & ( ) . , : ; ' ' ! ? * - — — [ ] † ‡ § ¶
Ta Te To Tr Tu Tw Ty Va Ve Vo Wa We
Wi Wo Wr Ya Ye Yo
⅛ ¼ ⅜ ½ ⅝ ¾ ⅞ ⅓ ⅔

[12] Font of 12-point Linotype Janson roman.

ABCDEFGHIJKLMNOPQRSTUVWXYZ
abcdefghijklmnopqrstuvwxyz
Æ Œ æ œ fi fl ff ffi ffl
AÁÄ EÉ IÍ
áàâäãāąåä çć éèêëēēē̄ê îìîïiï ńñ óòôöōŏô
ōō ŏŏ śş úùûiiūŭŭ
1234567890   1234567890
$ ℔ & ( ) , . : ; '' ! ?
Ta Te To Tr Tu Tw Ty Va Ve Vo Wa We
Wi Wo Wr Ya Ye Yo
gjpqy   gjpqy

[12a] Font of 12-point Linotype Janson italic.

The font that was used in the 42-line Bible of Gutenberg is believed to have included no less than 290 characters. This excessive number of variants on given letters was the result of Gutenberg's attempt to imitate the various nuances of ligatures (letters joined together and cast on a single body) and other special combinations in those contemporary manuscripts that were his models. This was a practice soon abandoned.

Hand Composition

The number of individual letters in a font will vary. The letters are cast according to the frequency of their use, and this, of course, varies with different languages. A font of type is stored in cases made up of numerous subdivisions. Two cases are usually required for a font. In one, there are CAPITALS, SMALL CAPITALS, and various special characters. In the second are the small letters (those descendants of the *scrittura umanistica*), numerals, and spacing material. The two cases are set one above the other on a sloping frame that usually serves as a storage cabinet and is sufficiently high to allow the compositor to work standing. From the working position of the two cases comes the common printer's terminology which refers to capitals as upper case and to the minuscules as lower case.

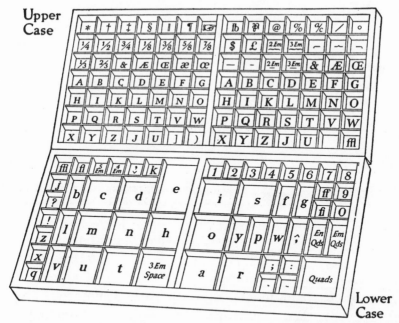

Upper Case

Lower Case

[13] Pair of printer's cases. Diagram by Rudolph Ruzicka for Updike's *Printing Types*.

A line of foundry type is still set, or composed, in a hand-held, adjustable frame called a *stick*, just as it has been for centuries. Since the letters are in reverse, right-to-left, they are assembled upside down to allow a right-left progression by the compositor. An adjustable stop on the stick is set to the line length required, and when the approximate maximum number of letters has been assembled, the line can be justified by adding spacing material. After several lines have been composed in the stick they are transferred to a long steel tray, open at one end, called a *galley*. Type is worked and stored in this form until made up into pages. The first proofs, made on long sheets of paper, are called galley proofs.

The Hand Press

Hand presses, such as the one Gutenberg developed, were platen presses, as were many of the later improved machines.

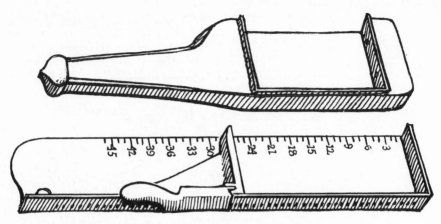

[14] Composing sticks: earliest type, single measure, made of wood; modern style, adjustable, made of steel.

Essentially, what is involved is the lowering of a heavy iron plate, the *platen*, under controlled pressure, against the horizontal, firmly backed type form. Although it is known that a cabinetmaker named Konrad Saspoch built Gutenberg's press, no detailed descriptions of it or other early models have survived. The general style of it is known, however, and is well illustrated in the reconstruction on exhibition at the Gutenberg Museum in Mainz. A fifteenth-century print shop is also effectively reproduced there.

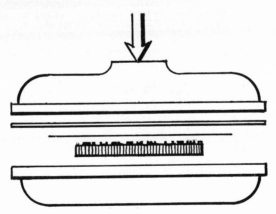

[15] Pressure system for letterpress printing.

[16] Gutenberg workshop. Reconstruction in the Gutenberg Museum.

CHAPTER III · *Type: Cutting and Casting*

The *bed* of the press is the part that holds the form for inking and printing. The type form is made up of pages locked into a metal frame, called a *chase*, by means of wooden or metal wedges, or *quoins*. Blank areas in a page or along margins are filled in with blocks known as *furniture*. The arrangement of the pages within the chase so that the printed pages will be in proper sequence for folding is the *imposing scheme*. A simple 16-page signature would be arranged in the chase thus:

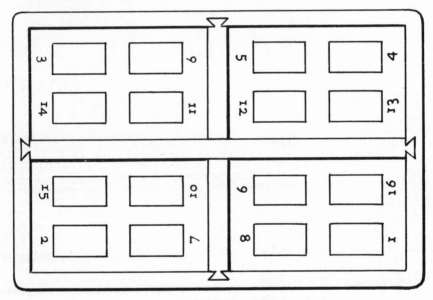

[17] Chase and lock-up of a sixteen-page form.

The bed is movable, on a track or forestay that allows it to be moved from under the platen and its lever-operated screw. The latter, much like the screw of a wine press, is steeply pitched to deliver its force through a minimum swing of the lever. Hinged to the bed is a frame, the *tympan*, on which paper can be stretched. This provides packing between the platen and the sheet which is to be printed. It is possible to build up areas on the tympan with thin layers of paper, and thus to adjust high and low areas in the type. This is called *overlay*. It also is possible to build up areas under the form, *underlay*. The whole is referred to as *make-ready*.

There is a second, hinged, unit, the *frisket*, which provides a shield to keep the printed sheet protected and clean. It is covered with paper and has a cut-out area equal to the type form. After the type has been inked with a pair of ink balls, a sheet of paper is laid on the tympan against preset guides. The frisket is closed over it, leaving exposed only that section of the paper that is to be printed on. It should be noted that it was customary to dampen paper for hand-press printing in order to counteract the sizing and soften the surface.

The bed assembly is moved under the platen and the lever pulled. Then the bed is moved out again, the tympan and frisket are lifted, and the paper is removed. This procedure is repeated for each impression. On the early presses pressure was so inadequate that it was sometimes necessary, when forms were large, to move the work piecemeal under the platen, employing a series of pulls on the lever.

It seems incredible that the numerous trials and failures, the ideas and the artifacts that led to the appearance of that first spectacular book to come from a press—Gutenberg's 42-line Bible—could have disappeared so completely. But it must be remembered that the scribes and illuminators wielded sufficient political power to have duplication of their works interdicted, except when done by hand. We have described both the clandestine exporting of prints and playing cards from Germany into Italy and the demand by Venetian woodcutters for legal protection. That was in 1441, just at the time that Gutenberg must surely have been at work on his ideas.

eos. Vnde eni̅ vocant̄ dij? Quia mulieres apponu̅t dijs argenteis et aure-
is ⁊ ligneis: ⁊ in domib₃ eo̅r sacerdotes sedent habentes tunicas sci̅ssas et
rapita ⁊ barbā rasam: quo̅r rapita
nuda sunt. Rugiu̅t aut damātes contra deos suos: sicut i̅ cena mortui. Ve-
stimenta eo̅r auferunt sacerdotes: et
vestiu̅t vxores suas ⁊ filios suos. Neq₃ si quid mali patiu̅tur ab aliquo neq₃ si quid boni poteru̅t retribuere: neq₃
regem co̅stituere possunt neq₃ auferre.
Similiter neq₃ dare diuitias possunt:
neq₃ malu̅ retribuere. Si q̅s illis vo-
tum vouerit ⁊ no̅ reddiderit: neq₃ hoc
requiru̅t. Homine̅ a morte no̅ librāt:
neq₃ infirmu̅ a potentiore eripiu̅t. Ho-
mine̅ cecu̅ ad visum non restituu̅t: de
necessitate homine̅ non liberabu̅t. Vi-
due non miserebu̅tur: neq₃ orphanis
bene facient. Lapidibus de mo̅te simi-
les sunt dij illo̅r lignei ⁊ lapidei ⁊ au-
rei et argentei: qui aut colu̅t ea co̅fun-
detur. Quomo̅ ergo estimādu̅ est aut
dicendu̅ illos esse deos? Adhuc enim
ipis caldeis non honorātibus ea: q̅
cum audierint mutu̅ non posse loqui
offeru̅t illud ad bel: postulātes ab eo
loqui: quasi possint sentire qui no̅ ha-
be̅t motu̅. Et ipi cu̅ intellexerint: relin-
quent ea. Sensum enim non habent
ipi dij illo̅r. Mulieres aut circu̅date
funib₃ in vijs sedent: succendētes ossa
oliuar̅. Cu̅ aut aliqua ex ipis abstra-
cta ab aliquo transeu̅te dormierit: pxi-
me sue exprobrat q̅ ea non sit digna
habita sicut ipa: neq₃ funis eius diru-
ptus sit. Om̅ia aut que illis fiu̅t falsa
sunt. Quomo̅ estimādu̅ aut dicendu̅
est illos esse deos? A fabris aut ⁊ au-
rificib₃ facta su̅t. Nichil aliud eru̅t nisi
id q̅d volu̅t esse sacerdotes. Aurifices

etiā ipi qui ea faciu̅t non sunt multi
temporis. Numquid ergo possunt ea q̅
fabricata su̅t ab ipis esse dij? Relique-
runt aut falsa et opprobriu̅ · postea fu-
turis. Nam cum superuenerit illis plu̅i̅
et mala: cogitant sacerdotes ubi se ab-
scondant cum illis. Quomo̅ ergo sen-
tiri debea̅t quoniā dij sunt qui nec de
bello se liberā̅t: neq₃ de malis se eripiu̅t?
Nam cum sint lignea et inaurata et
inargentata: scietur postea quia falsa
sunt ab oniu̅sis gentib₃ et regib₃ que
manifestata sunt quia non sunt dij:
sed opera manuu̅ hominu̅ · ⁊ nullu̅ op⁹
dei cu̅ illis. Vnde ergo notu̅ est q̅a non
su̅t dij: sed opera manuu̅ hoim: ⁊ nul-
lum dei op⁹ i̅ ipsis e̅. Rege̅ regioni no̅
suscitant: neq₃ pluuiā hominib₃ da-
bunt. Judiciu̅ quo̅q non discernent:
neq₃ regiones liberabunt ab iniuria:
quia nichil possunt sicut cornicule in-
ter mediu̅ celi et terre. Eteni̅ cu̅ incideret
ignis in domu̅ deo̅r ligneo̅r ⁊ argen-
teo̅r ⁊ aureo̅r: sacerdotes quide̅ ipso̅r
fugient et liberabuntur: ipi vero sicut
trabes i̅ medio co̅burentur. Regi aut
et bello no̅ resistent. Quomo̅ ergo esti-
mandu̅ e̅ aut recipiēdu̅ quia dij su̅t?
Non a furib₃ neq₃ a latronib₃ se libe-
rabu̅t dij lignei ⁊ lapidei ⁊ inaurati ⁊
inargētati: quib₃ iniqui fortiores su̅t.
Auru̅ et argentu̅ et vestime̅tu̅ quo o-
perti sunt auferent illis et abibu̅t: nec
sibi auxiliu̅ ferent. Itaq₃ melius est esse
regem ostentante̅ virtute̅ suā aut vas
in domo utile i̅ quo gloriabitur qui
possidet illud q̅ falsi dij: vel ostiu̅ i̅ domo q̅d custodit que in pace sunt: q̅
falsi dij. Sol quide̅ et luna ac sidera
cum sint splendida et emissa ad utili-
tates obaudiunt: similiter et fulgur
cu̅ apparuerit pspicuu̅ est. Idipm̅ aut

[1] Gutenberg Bible. The type page.

58

CHAPTER IV

The Incunabula: 1440—1500

THE WORD INCUNABULA comes from the Latin *cunae*, mean-ing "cradle." It can describe the earliest stages in the devel-opment of anything, but it has come to stand particularly for those books produced before 1500. The meager information about Gutenberg and his works at the time of his death has not been substantially added to since. His biography, as such, is based on fragile evidence, with many clues legal documents, detailing the indebtedness incurred while he was carrying on his experiments. He was born in Mainz, about the year 1397, and was the son of a member of the gentry, Friele zum Gens-fleisch. His name was Johann Gensfleisch zum Gutenberg. He lived in Mainz until 1428, when a dispute related to his guild caused him to move to Strasbourg. There he resided between 1434 and 1444, and worked with a goldsmith named Hans Duenne. It appears that he had begun his work with type as early as 1436. In 1439, in connection with a lawsuit, Duenne stated before a Strasbourg judge that Gutenberg had been en-gaged for three years on a project which had to do with print-ing. In 1438 Gutenberg was in possession of the press made to his specifications by Konrad Saspoch and was purchasing lead; this suggests that he had reached the stage of casting. The last record of Gutenberg's presence in Strasbourg is a tax payment in 1444.

The 42-Line Bible

By 1448 he had returned to Mainz and had obtained a loan of 150 gulden from a relative there. This was insufficient for his needs since he was again seeking financial backing only two years later. This time he borrowed 800 gulden, at 6 per cent interest, from Johann Fust, a wealthy Mainz merchant. The loan was secured by a mortgage on Gutenberg's equipment. After still another borrowing, the agreement was foreclosed. By that time, 1455, the loans and interest had reached more than 2,000 gulden, a sum Gutenberg was unable to pay. His books and tools were forfeited to satisfy the debt. The irony of this misfortune lay in the imminent appearance of his great 42-line Bible.

[2] Gutenberg Bible. The type.

In retrospect, Gutenberg's accomplishment ranks with the major innovations of history. Within a few decades after his Bible was printed, presses began to produce the grammars and dictionaries that were to be the basic tools for increasing literacy. Vespasiano, with fifty-five writers working for him, needed almost two years to finish two hundred books. Froben was able to print 24,000 copies of Erasmus' *Colloquies* in a few months.

Our own ideas of the importance of the press embrace all its uses. Some of these uses, such as newspapers, were merely seed in the impressions that were pulled in Gutenberg's workshop in Mainz. It seems inconceivable that the man who was responsible for such a seminal contribution as movable type could remain a shadowy figure in the pages of history.

At this point in Gutenberg's story, it is necessary to turn from him and to learn something of the man who would help Fust carry on the Gutenberg venture. His name was Peter

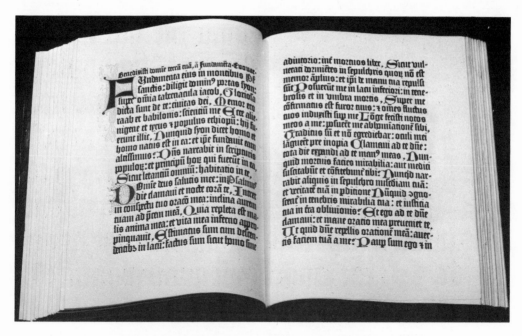

[3] The Mainz Psalter of Fust and Schöffer.

Schöffer and he was a calligrapher who was working in Paris at the beginning of the second half of the fifteenth century. From Paris he moved to Mainz, where he met and married Fust's daughter. He designed and cast type, and became first a working partner and later the heir of Fust.

Fust and Schöffer

Shortly after the appearance of Gutenberg's big Bible, the large and handsome Mainz Psalter was published in 1457. It bore the first colophon, giving the date of publication and the names of Fust and Schöffer as its publishers. On the basis of the time required to complete such an undertaking, it would seem that at least some of the initial work on it had been done by Gutenberg.

Among the notable features of the Mainz Psalter were its large two-color printed initials. This feat was probably done by preparing the wood blocks in such a way that they could be separated and lifted for individual inking in red and blue. The form could then be printed in one impression.

[4] Initial. Mainz Psalter.

The type used in both Bible and Psalter was a gothic *lettre de forme*, which was called *Textur* by the Germans. This simply means texture, and application of the word to gothic type stemmed from the woven appearance of a page executed in such a letter style. In both these books the types are large in size, especially in the body of the Latin Psalter, and they have the same angular, pointed style. As examples of Textur Gothic, they are exemplary in their simplicity of conception. Although extremely pointed, they were less *spiky* than many similar forms which were to follow.

The lines from the Fust and Schöffer Psalter reproduced below show two sizes of type. In the smaller size, capitals

[5] Type. Mainz Psalter.

A Short History of the Printed Word

appear and they are characteristic of the letter. These capitals are generous in their forms, especially against the close-packed vertical rhythm of the lower case. The lines, dots, and other decorative touches are not solely for ornament; they help to reduce the large counters which could otherwise open up holes in the over-all texture and color of the type mass.

The large, decorative letters, which are below in the body of the text, are in a style known as *versals*. In manuscripts, they were compound, or built-up, forms. On this page, they indicate the degree to which the early printers were committed to imitating the illuminators as well as the calligraphers. Naturally, these letters also serve their practical purposes of indicating textual breaks and stresses.

[5a] Type. *Hortus Sanitatis.*

Peter Schöffer was to have a long and productive life; not so his benefactor, Fust, who died of the plague in 1466 in Paris. Two of Schöffer's most famous works—the *Hortus Sanitatis*, an herbal in German, and *Chronik der Sachsen*—did not appear until 1485 and 1492. Both were extensively illustrated with woodcuts.

After his death in 1502, Peter Schöffer was succeeded by his son, Johann, and finally by Ivo Schöffer, who may also have been a son, and who continued printing until 1555. Thus, the name Schöffer was associated for a full century with the making of books.

The Death of Gutenberg

Gutenberg did not outlast Fust by very long, dying in 1468. Little is known about his later years until 1465, when he became attached to the court of Adolf of Nassau, Archbishop of Mainz. In 1460 there appeared, printed in Mainz, the *Catholicon*, a Latin dictionary written by Johann Balbus in the late thirteenth century. Although proof is lacking, this book has been attributed to Gutenberg.

In February of 1468, Dr. Conrad Humery, a Mainz advocate, recorded his acquisition of some printing equipment that had belonged to Gutenberg at the time of his death. These articles were turned over to Humery by the Archbishop, and it may be assumed that the doctor had been of some economic help to the always financially embarrassed inventor-printer.

Exodus of the Mainz Printers

In 1462, Mainz was attacked, sacked, and partly burned by soldiers of the Archbishop of Nassau. One consequence of that disruption of commerce was an exodus of some of the printers from the city, thus hastening the spread of the infant art to other towns and countries. In that decade, there were presses in Strasbourg and Bamberg. It was in Bamberg, in 1461, that Albrecht Pfister printed *Edelstein*, the first illustrated book. The woodcut illustrations were printed as a separate impression.

Four years later the art moved into Italy, when Sweynheym and Pannartz set up a shop in the monastery at Subiaco, near Rome. In 1466, there was printing in Cologne, in 1468 in Augsburg and Rome. The following year, Johannes da Spira became the first Venetian printer. Then, in 1470, a particularly significant year, a printing office was started at the Sorbonne, the Rector having invited three German printers to Paris. In

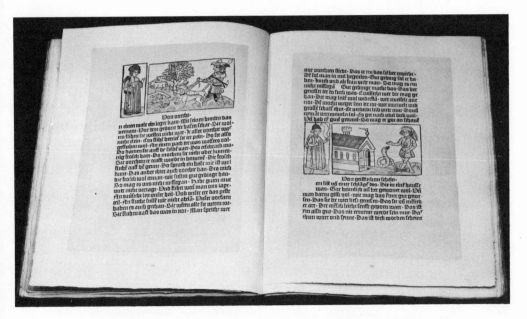

[6] The first illustrated book: *Edelstein,* by Albrecht Pfister.

Venice the great Nicolas Jenson began his influential Italian career.

The Mainz influence was dominant for the first fifteen years of bookmaking. Type men from other countries, such as Schöffer and Jenson from France, were apprenticed at Mainz. The exodus from that city, in 1462, must have been greatly governed by the demand for printing elsewhere. The supply of trained craftsmen was relatively small.

Subiaco

For these printers, protection and financial support guaranteed success. Since the churches were among the principal customers for books, their language chiefly Latin (which the Germans were already used to), and their means ample, they offered the most ideal inducements. Just such a set of circumstances was present in the case of Conrad Sweynheym and Arnold Pannartz, the Germans who introduced printing to Italy in 1465. Their press was set up at the Benedictine house, Santa Scholastica, at Subiaco. After producing a Donatus, of which no copy is extant, they printed *De Divinis Institutioni-*

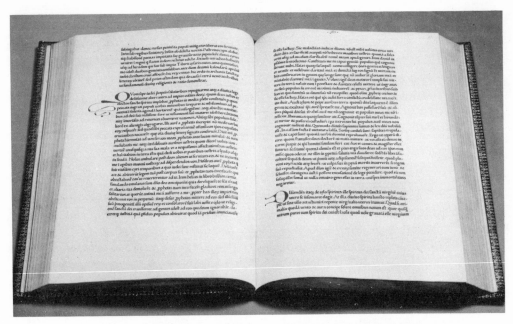

[7] Lactantius *Opera*. 1465. Sweynheym and Pannartz.

bus of Lactantius, which was the first Italian book to bear a date. Sweynheym was a Mainz clerk who had worked for Schöffer, and Pannartz is known to have been a native of Cologne.

Johann Zainer became the first printer in Ulm. In 1473, he brought out Boccaccio's *De Claris Mulieribus*, illustrated with woodcuts based on French manuscript illumination. Johann Zainer is also noted for his efforts in utilizing scholarship in the preparation of his publications.

agit̃. ut huana diuinis tribuãt auctoritatẽ: cũ pocius huma
buerĩt. Quę nũc fane omittamus. ne nihil apud iftos agar
materia‚pcedat. Ea igr quęramus teftimonia.qbus illi poffi
aut certe non repugnare. Sibillas plurimi et maximi auctͨ
gręcoʒ: Ariftoricus: et Appollodorus: Erithreus: noftro̊
neftella. Hi omes pcipuam et nobilem pręter cęteras. Erith
memorãt. Appollodorus qdẽ ut de ciui ac populari fua glc

[8] Type of Sweynheym and Pannartz. 1465

A Short History of the Printed Word

The type used by Sweynheym and Pannartz was strongly influenced by the *scrittura umanistica* and bears gothic traces. Despite that, it is considered to be the first roman type. The capitals are roman, and the lines are spaced more widely than in gothic. Both these factors help to increase the roman *mise en page* of the Subiaco type. Aside from the Donatus and the Lactantius, only two other books were printed at Subiaco. These were Cicero's *De Oratore* and St. Augustine's *De Civitate Dei*. The Cicero is thought to have been completed first, but it is undated. After printing the St. Augustine, Sweynheym and Pannartz moved their press to the palace of the de' Massimi family in Rome. There, they printed about fifty books, working together until 1473.

Printing in Switzerland and Germany

In 1463, at Mainz, Fust and Schöffer printed the first book to have a title page. The following year, a Gutenberg workman named Berthold Ruppel went to Basel and became Switzerland's first printer. Another Zainer, Günther, a Strasbourg printer, moved his press to Augsburg in 1468. It was to become one of the great printing centers of Germany, due in some degree to Zainer. Encountering the opposition of local woodcutters and block-printers, who greatly feared his competition, Zainer was fortunate enough to have the interested support of Melchior von Stamhaim, Abbot of St. Ulrich, who offered him room for his press. In a few years, five presses were added and under Zainer's tutelage printers were trained. The first book to come from his press was *Meditationes de Vita Christi*. Zainer used many woodcuts in his books, and it is reasonable to assume that the fearful wood-carvers and playing-card makers were soon absorbed into the new operation, with greatly expanded duties and opportunities. The demands were to elevate the craft for several hundred years to come.

The first book printed in Venice was completed in 1469. It was *Epistolae ad Familiares* by Cicero and its printer the German Johannes da Spira. It was followed by Pliny's *Historia*

S Ed neceſſe eſt inquiunt: ut terrena corpora natur
teneat: uel cogat ad terram: & ideo in caelo eſſe non po
illi homiés in terra erant nemoroſa atque fructuoſa: ‹
obtinuit.Sed quia & ad hoc reſpondendū eſt:uel propt
quo aſcendit in caelum:uel propter ſanctorum qualia ii
ſunt: intueantur paulo attentius pondera ipá terrena.
efficit: ut ex metallis que in aquis poſita continuo ſubi

[9] Type of Johannes and Wendelin da Spira. 1470

Naturalis. In 1470, in association with his brother, Wendelin,
Da Spira issued *De Civitate Dei*, the first book to have page
folios (numbers). Johannes died that year and was succeeded
by Wendelin.

Printing in Venice

The type used by the Da Spiras was of an extraordinary
character: roman forms that are completely recognizable as
such by modern standards. The brothers made great claims for
their designs as being, in fact, an invention, and they were able
to obtain protection against plagiarism for five years.

The death of Johannes da Spira in 1470 removed that restriction, and in that year there appeared Eusebius' *De Praepa-
ratione Evangelica*, a milestone in the development of the roman
type page. This is called the first book by Nicolas Jenson, but
there are reasons to believe that he was the author of the Da
Spira roman type. Since Jenson was one of the great seminal
punch-cutters, it is a more logical assumption than to accept the
alternative conclusion that he leaned heavily on his predecessor
for inspiration.

Nicolas Jenson

Jenson was born at Sommevaire, France, in 1420. Between
1470 and 1480 he printed some 150 books and established a

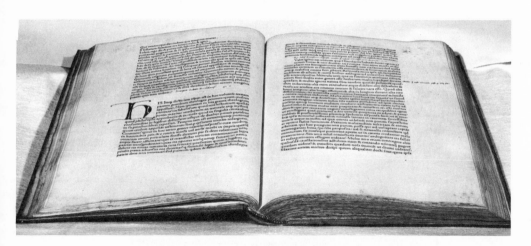

[10] Eusebius by Nicolas Jenson. 1470.

lasting reputation for his types. He has been identified as a mintmaster, at Tours or Paris. One version of his life places him in 1458 in Mainz, sent by King Charles VII to learn the craft of type-making and printing. The King died in 1461, and for some reason Jenson met with the vindictive opposition of the new ruler, Louis XI. As a result, he did not return to France.

The man who produced the Eusebius type did not suddenly achieve the mastery manifest in that font. There are clues connecting Jenson with Frankfurt, and some which place Gutenberg there from the time he lost his equipment in Mainz until 1468. Thus it is possible to build a case for Jenson's having had direct contact with Gutenberg. Certainly, Jenson was associated with Frankfurt merchants, especially with booksellers. One of these, Peter Ugelheimer, who had a connection with the book business as early as 1455, appears in Venice twenty years later, at the height of Jenson's Italian career. It is also of interest to note that among the shareholders in Jenson's last partnership were Donna Paula, the widow of Johannes da Spira, and her two children. The presence of the three lends great weight to the theory that Jenson cut the punches for the da Spira roman. He died in Rome in 1480, having gone there at the invitation of Pope Sixtus IV.

Jenson was a success in his own time, both artistically and financially. Beyond his time, he was an inspiration to generations to come. It is my belief that his influence came partly

qui omnibus uı aquarum fubmerſis cum filiis ſuis ſimul ac nuribus
mirabili quodā modo quaſi ſemen huāni generis conſeruatus eſt:quē
utinā quaſi uiuam quandam imaginem ımıtari nobis contıngat:& hi
quidem ante diluuium fuerunt:poſt diluuium autem alii quorū unus
altıſſimi dei ſacerdos iuſtitiæ ac pietatis miraculo rex iuſtus lıngua he⸗
bræorū appellatus eſt:apud quos nec circuncıſionis nec moſaıcæ legis
ulla mentıo erat . Quare nec ıudæos(poſteris enı hoc nomen fuit)neqʒ
gentıles:quoniam non ut gentes pluralitatem deorum inducebant ſed
hebræos proprie noıamus aut ab Hebere ut dıctū eſt:aut qa ıd nomen
tranſitiuos ſignificat.Soli qppe a creaturıs naturalı rōne & lege ınata
nō ſcrıpta ad cognitionē ueri dei trāſiere:& uoluptate corporıs cōtépta
ad rectam uitam pueniſſe ſcribunt:cum quibus omıbus præclarus ılle
totius generis origo Habraam numerādus eſt:cui ſcriptura mirabilem
iuſtitıā quā non a moſaica lege(ſeptima eīm poſt Habraā generatione
Moyſes naſcitur)ſed naturalı fuit ratione conſecutus ſūma cum laude
atteſtatur.Credidit enim Habraam deo & reputatū eſt ei in iuſtitiam.
Quare multarum quoqʒ gentium patrem dıuina oracula futurū:ac ın
ıpſo benedicēdas oēs gentes hoc uıdelıc& ıpſum quod iam nos uıdeūs
aperte prædictum eſt:cuius ille iuſtitiæ perfectioém non moſaıca lege
ſed fide cōſecutus eſt:qui poſt multas dei uiſiones legittimum genuıt
filium:quem primum omnium diuino pſuaſus oraculo circūcıdit:&
cæteris qui ab eo naſcerétur tradidit:uel ad manifeſtum multıtudinis
eorum futuræ ſignum:uel ut hoc quaſi paternæ uirtutis īſigne filıı re⸗
tinētes maiores ſuos ımitari conaret:aut qbuſcūqʒ aliıs de cauſis.Non
enim ıd ſcrutādum nobis modo eſt.Poſt Habraam filius eius Iſaac in
pietate ſucceſſit:fœlice hac hæreditate a parétibus accæpta:q unı uxori
coniunctus quum geminos genuiſſet caſtitatis amore ab uxore poſtea
dicitur abſtinuiſſe.Ab iſto natus ē Iacob qui ͵ppter cumulatū uirtutis
prouétum Iſrael etiam appellatus eſt duobus noībus ͵ppter duplicem
uirtutis uſū.Iacob eīm athletā & exercétem ſe latıne dicere poſſumus:
quam appellationé primū habuit:quū practicis operatıoībus multos
pro pietate labores ferebat.Quum auté iam uictor luctando euaſit:&
ſpeculationis fruebat͗bonis:tūc Iſraelem ipſe deus appellauit æterna
premia beatitudıneqʒ ultimam quæ in uiſione dei conſıſtit eı largiens:
hominem enim quı deum uideat Iſrael nomen ſignificat. Ab hoc.xii.
iudæorum tribus ͵pfectæ ſūt.Innumerabilia de uıta ıſtorum uirorum
fortitudine prudentia pietateqʒ dıci poſſunt:quorum alia ſecundum
ſcripturæ uerba hiſtorice conſiderantur:alia tropologice ac allegorice
interpretāt͗:de qbus multi cōſcripſerūt:& nos in libro qué inſcripſiūs

[11] Jenson. Text page from Eusebius.

Et picis in morem ad digitos lentefcit habendo. Eiufmodi
figuratio parum admifit ex fe perfectum:nec conuenit ad
mittere ut aut poffit:aut debeat cum cæteris temporibus p
totam declinationem uim incipiendi fignificare . Abfurdū
ē ergo ea quæ funt inchoatiua perfecto tempore definire:&
mox futurum declinando inchoatiua effe demōftrare·Nec
enim poteftcum tota uerbi fpecies inchoatiua dicatur alia

[12] Type of Nicolas Jenson. 1471.

from early training, which gave him even greater sensitivity to
the sculptural nature of type than was natural for the average
goldsmith-turned-punch-cutter. In making coins and medal-
lions, the letter forms Jenson employed were capitals, often
beautiful capitals that could summon the spirit of Rome. It is
reasonable to assume that Jenson's Latin background and his
proficiency in roman forms were of incalculable importance in
translating humanistic script from a calligraphic expression into
type.

To those who would point to a lack of perfection in detail
in Jenson's type, the answer should stand plainly on a page
where the even color of the type mass and the great legibility of
the forms speak for the successful achievement of the printer's
aims. Dressmaker details and elegant touches do not bear constant repetition. It is the elusive inevitability of Jenson's forms
that has made them models for nearly five hundred years. Part
of the character of a Jenson page derives from the fitting of the
letters; there is sufficient space between them to match the
space within the counters.

In 1471, Jenson produced a Greek type, for use in quota-
tions, and in 1473 a gothic font, for his expanding production
of medical and historical works. However, his fame has rested
on his contribution to the form of roman type and the way it
could be composed and arranged on a page.

In spite of the success of the Venetian printers, Florentine
bibliophiles remained aloof in their attitude toward the press. It
was a time of high attainment by their calligraphic school, well

represented by the work of Antonio Sinibaldi. The first book printed in Florence was produced by a goldsmith, in 1472. It was indifferent in quality. In fact, that great center of art was generations away from the level of printing of which it should have been the master.

The Spread of Printing: Spain and Holland

From 1450 or thereabouts until 1470, fourteen cities could boast printing offices. From 1470 to 1480, the number had grown to more than one hundred. Of that number, Italy accounted for forty-seven. In France, besides the three Germans, Friburger, Gering, and Krantz, who had been called to the Sorbonne in 1470, there were printers at Toulouse, Angers, Vienne, Poitiers, and, most importantly, at Lyons.

Printing was introduced into Spain, at Valencia, in 1474. From then, to the end of the decade, presses were established in Saragossa, Tortosa, Seville, Barcelona, and Lerida. Lambert Palmart was the first Spanish printer and Matthaeus of Flanders the second. In Spain, as elsewhere, the spread of printing was carried on by itinerant Germans, that is, German by training if not by birth. The state of the art was no longer tentative, and an industry had come into being. Despite the nationality of the earliest printers in Spain, their products rapidly took on a recognizable Spanish style. It can be said, too, that the craft was embraced by the people.

The Spaniards quickly asserted their preference for gothics, in their case the round gothic called *rotunda*. Juan de Yciar's *Arte Subtilissima*, a writing-book published in 1550 at Saragossa, shows this form to best advantage. It would seem that foreign influences either succumbed to the strong nationalism of Spain or were at least absorbed into it.

Despite the claims of Holland as the land where printing began and of Coster as the man who began it, 1473 is the earliest firm date for Dutch printing. This date is established by two books, produced in Utrecht in that year, by Ketelaer and de Leempt. There are some undated works, presumed to have

[13] Round gothic by Juan de Yciar.

been printed several years before, perhaps as early as 1471. About four years after the Utrecht books appeared, printing shops were opened in Deventer, Delft, and Gouda. During the remaining years of that decade, four more shops appeared.

William Caxton

In the 1470's, printing was also introduced in neighboring Belgium. The first press was at Alost, in 1473. After that, printing was undertaken in Louvain, Bruges, Brussels, and, by 1480, at Audenarde. It was at Bruges, in 1475, that William Caxton printed the first book in English. It was his own translation of *Le Recueil des Histoires de Troyes*, and he called it *Recuyell of the Historyes of Troye*.

Caxton was born about 1422. In 1438, he was apprenticed to the wealthy Robert Large, soon to be Lord Mayor of London, and there made those connections which were to be so

Jn the tyme of p troublous worldͬ/ and of the
hons beyng andͬ reygnyng as well m the roʒ
englondͬ andͬ fraunce as m all other places vͬ
thurgh the worldͬ that is to wete the yere of oꭜ
thousandͬ four hondͬerdͬ lꭓꭓi . Andͬ asfoꭜ the tꭜ
whiche tretͬeth of the generall ᷍ lastͬ destruccōn

[14] Type of Caxton's first book in English.

helpful in advancing his second career as printer-publisher. In
the 1440's, he was in business in Bruges. Within a dozen years
he was prominent in the Mercers' Company, rising to the gov-
ernorship of the Guild of English Merchants which was
formed within the Mercers' Company. He held that office for a
number of years, exercising powers similar to those of a magis-
trate or a judge.

Caxton's translation of the Le Fèvre *Recueil,* which was
begun in 1469, had been laid aside, but while he was secretary
to Margaret of Burgundy, he was persuaded by her to resume
the work. This he did in 1471 in Cologne, where he became
interested in printing. He is thought to have learned the craft
from Ulrich Zell, a priest from Mainz who had established
Cologne's first press. On returning to Bruges, Caxton set up a
press to print his book. To do this, he asked a calligrapher,
Colard Mansion, to join him in his project. The type they used
was a cursive gothic, of the style called *bâtarde,* closely related
to a Flemish hand. Its features are pointed descenders, looped
ascenders, the italic-like *a,* and the open-tailed *g.*

In 1476, Caxton returned to England. His press, at the Sign
of the Red Pale, was situated at Westminster, near the Abbey.
There, in 1477, he printed his first dated work: *The Dictes or
Sayengis of the Philosophres.* Before his death in 1491, Caxton
had printed ninety-six to one hundred works. It is interesting to
speculate how the style of English and American printing
might have developed if Caxton had learned to work type, and
to print from it, in Italy or France. Had he done so, there might

suspect persone ¶ And sayd, the wele disposed man re-
membreth but his synnes, and the euyl disposed hath
mynde but on his vertues. It fortuned his wyf was deces-
sed in a ferre countre, and som ayed him If there were
eny differrence to dye in their propre lande or ellis ferre from
thens. The answerd, Wheresomeuer one dye, the weye to the
other worlde is all like ¶ And sayd to a yong man that
wolde not lerne in his yought, If thou wolt not take peyne
to lerne thou shalt haue the peyne to be lewde, and vncon-
nyng ¶ And sayd god loueth thoos that bee disobeissaunt
to euyl temptacion ¶ And sayd, good prayer is one of
the beste thinges a man may present to god, and if thou axe
him ony boon lete thy werkis be agreable vnto him

Dyogenes otherwyse called dogly bycause he hadde
som condicions of a dogge, and he was the wysest
man that was in his dayes. He dispraised grete-
ly the worlde, and lay in a tonne, Whiche he tourned for
his auantage from the sonne. And the wynde, as it plea-
sed hym, and therin he rested Whansomeuer the nyght fil
vpon him. He ete Whansomeuer he was hungred, Were it
by day or by nyght in the strete or ellis Where Wythoute eny
shame therof. And was content Wyth .ij. gownes of
wollen cloth in the yere. And so he keupd and gouuer-
ned him self til his deth. Somme ayed him Why he
was called dogly, he sayd be cause I barke vpon the foo-
les and falle vpon the wysemen. Alexandre the grete
cam vnto him of whom he toke litle regarde, he ayed him
Why he sette so litil by him, seeyng that he was so mighty a
kyng and hadde noo necessite, he answerd I haue noght to

[15] Caxton's first dated work in England: *The Dictes or
Sayengis of the Philosophres*. 1477.

have been an earlier release from the thralldom of the black
letter, not to mention an initial appreciation of the full resources of roman. However, he did present England with a
model for her printer-publishers, combining as he did scholarship, craftsmanship, dedication, and enough business acumen to
make the enterprises pay. He was followed by his assistant,
Wynkyn de Worde.

CHAPTER IV · *The Incunabula: 1440–1500* 75

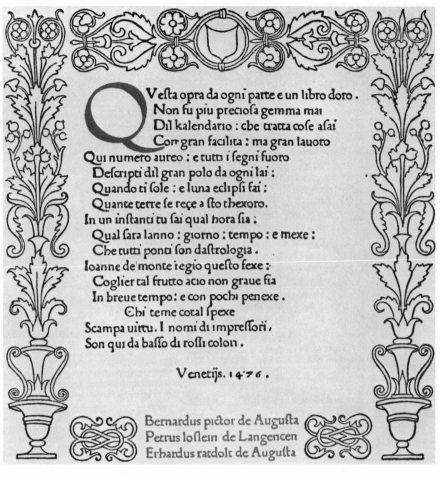

Vesta opra da ogni parte e un libro doro.
Non fu piu preciosa gemma mai
Dil kalendario : cbe tratta cose asai
Con gran facilita : ma gran lauoro
Qui numero aureo : e tutti i segni fuoro
Descripti dil gran polo da ogni lai :
Quando ti sole : e luna eclipsi sai :
Quante terre se rece a sto thexoro.
In un instanti tu sai qual hora sia :
Qual sara lanno : giorno : tempo : e mexe :
Che tutti ponti son dastrologia .
Ioanne de monte regio questo fexe :
Coglier tal frutto acio non graue sia
In breue tempo: e con pochi penexe .
Chi teme cotal spexe
Scampa uittu. I nomi di impressori ,
Son qui da basso di rossi colori .

Venetijs. 1476 .

Bernardus pictor de Augusta
Petrus loslein de Langencen
Erhardus ratdolt de Augusta

[16] Ratdolt, Loeslein, and Maler. *Kalendarius.* 1476.

Erhard Ratdolt

In the years when Caxton was printing his first book at Westminster, Erhard Ratdolt was at work in Venice, 1476–86. His were the first decorative title pages and the first mathematical diagrams. The diagrams appeared in his *Elementa Geometriae* of Euclid. He also was an innovator in the printing of multicolor woodcuts. Above all, he was responsible for some of the outstanding books, in both appearance and execution, which were printed in Venice, where the work was considered to be a model for all Europe. Ratdolt might have been just the partner for Caxton's English establishment. He did have part-

A Short History of the Printed Word

ners of his own; their names, Peter Loeslein and Bernhart (Bernardus) Maler, appeared with Ratdolt's on the proto title page of their *Kalendarius* of 1476. Maler probably designed and cut the decorative material. Ratdolt returned to his native city, Augsburg, in 1486. He there printed his handsome and famous type-specimen sheet, the first instance of such a showing by a printer. In Augsburg he continued to work for more than thirty years, and died there in 1528 at the age of eighty-one.

Late Fifteenth-Century Printing in England and France

During the final twenty years of the fifteenth century, nearly 140 towns were added to those having presses. Among the important centers for printing were London, Leipzig, Munich, Stockholm, Lisbon, Hamburg, and Copenhagen. In London, John Letton, William de Machlinia, and Richard Pynson were early printers. Pynson deserves special mention for several reasons. First, he had a sense of style that raised him above other English printers of the fifteenth century; second, he is credited with introducing roman type into England early in the following century; and third, he was memorialized by the late Elmer Adler, the influential American typographer, in the naming of his press, Pynson Printers.

Pynson was born in Normandy and learned printing in Rouen. He took over the shop of De Machlinia about 1490. In 1494 he issued Boccaccio's *Fall of the Princes*, in a translation by John Lydgate. He continued working until 1528, two years before his death.

Of the three printers who began in France, at the Sorbonne, in 1470, two, Friburger and Krantz, returned to Germany in 1477. The third, Ulrich Gering, remained. He was joined later by Berthold Rembolt, and their office continued to make significant contributions to printing until the end of the century. From the standpoint of activity, Lyons came close to matching Paris. Like Venice, Lyons was a great commercial center. It also enjoyed a great freedom from restrictions imposed by

[17] Philippe Pigouchet. *Livre d'Heures*. 1498.

ecclesiastical censorship. Guillaume Le Roy introduced printing in Lyons in 1473. Five years later, the first French illustrated book, *Le Mirouer de la Rédemption*, was printed in
Lyons, using types and woodcuts imported from Basel. For
most of the French books printed in the fifteenth century,
gothic letters were used. After the first use of roman, at the
Sorbonne, it fell into disfavor until later in the century. There
were pointed gothics, round gothics, and especially the cursive
vernacular *lettres bâtarde*.

A Short History of the Printed Word

[18] *St. Christopher on Horseback*. Metal cut executed about 1475 with gravers and punches. The technique, called *manière criblée*, is related to the *niello* work of goldsmiths.

Among the notable aspects of French manuscript production were the *Horae*, or Books of Hours. The writing and illumination of such books provided some of the most magnificent examples of French calligraphy and miniature painting. Several French printers, it would seem, set out to match that achievement in type and woodcuts. One of these, Philippe

[19] Albrecht Dürer. Woodcut, *Apocalypse*. 1498.

Pigouchet, whose *Livre d'Heures* was printed in 1498 at Paris, is an excellent representative of the group. In the following century, this specialty was to continue and to reach its height in the hands of Geofroy Tory.

Albrecht Dürer and Aldus Manutius

As always happens with a new medium, printing was beginning to develop and perfect its own practitioners. This was

A Short History of the Printed Word

[20] Aldus. *Hypnerotomachia Poliphili.* 1499.

especially true of woodcutting and there is no more spectacular example than the magnificent cuts made by Albrecht Dürer in 1498 for the *Apocalypse*, printed in Nuremberg by Anton Koberger. They represent a great esthetic achievement as well as a technical one. In a very different style, a set of woodcut illustrations made in Venice for Colonna's *Hypnerotomachia Poliphili*, and printed by Aldus Manutius in 1499, succeeds in epitomizing the harmony between type and decorative illustration. Both of these books seem to begin the sixteenth century, rather than to end the fifteenth.

Perhaps no one better could be chosen to close the period of the incunabula than Aldus Manutius, the Latin name for Teobaldo Mannucci, who was born in Sermoneta, Italy. His studies at Ferrara and Rome included Greek, and he hoped to use printing in a revival of classical wisdom. After finding a patron, he established himself in Venice in 1494 and founded the Aldine Press. As a printer's mark, he used the dolphin and anchor, one of the many symbols for the popular Renaissance motto "Make haste slowly."

Aldus invited scholars of Greek to live with him; the most

EL SEQVENTE triúpho nõ meno mirauegliofo dl primo. Impo che egli hauea le q̃tro uolubile rote tutte, & gli radii, & il meditullo defu fco achate, di cádide uéule uagaméte uaricato. Ne tale certaínte geftoe re Pyrrho cũ le noue Mufe & Apolline i medio pulfáte dalla natura ípffo.

Laxide & la forma del dicto q̃le el primo, ma le tabelle eráo di cyaneo Saphyro orientale, atomato de fcintillule doro, alla magica gratiffimo, & longo acceptiffimo a cupidine nella finiftra mano.

Nella tabella dextra mirai exfcalpto una infigne Matróa che dui oui hauea parturito, in uno cubile regio colloca ta, di uno mirabile pallacio, Cum obftetrice ftu pefacte, & multe altre matrone & aftante NympheDegli quali ufciua de uno una flammula, & delal tro ouo due fpectatiffi me ftelle.

* *
*

[20a] Type page of the *Hypnerotomachia Poliphili*.

distinguished of these was Erasmus. Important in the history of printing types was his employment of Francesco Griffo of Bologna, an independent punch-cutter, to produce the roman first used in Bembo's *De Aetna* in 1495. Griffo also cut the first italic, that lower-case alphabet based on a chancery hand. His third roman font for Aldus was that used in the *Hypnerotomachia Poliphili*. The special innovation of Aldus and Griffo, in the romans, was their use of the calligraphic practice of making the capitals shorter than the ascending letters of the lower case.

A Short History of the Printed Word

NARRA QVIVI LA DIVA POLIA LA NOBILE ET
ANTIQVA ORIGINE SVA.ET COMO PER LI PREDE
CESSORI SVI TRIVISIO FVE EDIFICATO.ET DI QVEL
LA GENTE LELIA ORIVNDA. ET PER QVALE MO
DO DISAVEDVTA ET INSCIA DISCONCIAMENTE
SE INAMOROE DI LEI IL SVO DILECTO POLIPHILO.

E MIE DEBILE VOCE TALE O GRA
tiofe & diue Nymphe abfone perueneráno &
inconcíne alla uoftra benigna audiétia . quale
la terrifica raucitate del urinante Efacho al fua-
ue canto dela piangeuole Philomela. Nondi
meno uolendo io cum tuti gli mei exili cona-
ti del intellecto,& cum la mia paucula fufficié
tia di fatiffare alle uoftre piaceuole petitione,
non riftaro al potere. Lequale femota qualúque hefitatione epfe piu che
fi congruerebbe altronde, dignamente meritano piu uberrimo fluuio di
eloquentia , cum troppo piu rotunda elegantia & cum piu exornata poli

[21] Type of Aldus's *Hypnerotomachia Poliphili.* 1499.

This corrected one of the color problems of Jenson's types: a
tendency of the large capitals to be spotty in the type mass.

As the fifteenth century ended, printing was well established, but calligraphy was by no means a dying influence.
Some of its most beautiful examples were still ahead. As more
people learned to read, more learned to write, and often with
great style and distinction. The sixteenth century was the age
of the great manuals for handwriting.

CHAPTER V

The Sixteenth Century

AN INVENTORY of the physical and material progress of print-ing until the year 1500 would reveal more than 1,100 shops in 200 cities, in which some 12,000,000 books, in 35,000 editions, had been produced. On the esthetic side, the high state of calligraphy during that period provided an atmosphere of understanding and taste for letter forms that has been of lasting benefit in establishing the classic models for type families. Me-chanically, very little had changed since the time of Gutenberg. The appearance of technical progress stemmed from increased skill in the craft. For instance, Peter Schöffer died in 1502. He had relinquished control of his shop some years earlier. Nev-ertheless, he represented, in one lifespan, the full course of printing history, with all the experience that implies. In 1500, presses still used wooden screws to deliver the force for the impressions. It was not until 1550 that a Nuremberg mechanic made a metal thread for the power action.

In the new century, printing was to spread to ten countries: Turkey, 1503; Rumania, 1508; Greece, 1515; Mexico, 1534; Ireland, 1550; Russia, 1553; India, 1556; Palestine, 1563; Peru, 1584; Japan, 1590. To Americans, it should be especially inter-esting that Mexico had a printing press a full century before the one set up in North America, at Cambridge, Massachusetts. The religious, political, social, and economic ferment that marked the sixteenth century is well known; the economic and social structure of the Middle Ages was being challenged in every aspect. It was the century of Luther and Calvin, of the Peasants' War and the Knights' War. The first printing of Martin Luther's translation of the New Testament, with illus-trations by the elder Cranach, was completed in 1522. It is not

[1] Aldus. *Virgil* of 1501.

too much to say that the tool of change was the press, and that this change, in turn, helped to spread printing.

The Introduction of Italic

When Aldus commissioned a cursive type based on the *cancellaresca*, or chancery script, imitating Italian vernacular handwriting, one purpose was to produce a condensed letter for use in small formats which might "more conveniently be held in the hand and learned by heart." Another purpose was to duplicate the type texture of his cursive Greek fonts. The books were a Virgil and a Juvenal, the year was 1501, the punch-cutter was Francesco Griffo of Bologna, and the result was italic.

The chancery script was being written with greatest distinction at the time of the first books printed in italic type. No one was more masterly in the writing of this script than Raphael. Shortly before he was made painter at the palace of Pope Julius II, he had been nominated for a papal secretaryship.

carissimo quanto padre Io ho receuto una uostra letera p la quale ho inteso la morte del nostro S.
amico a laquale ano aui misiuicordia alamma e certo nõ fiabile senza lacrime legere lauostra lete[ra]
ma transeat aquello nõ a e rigore bisogna auere patientia encardaansi con lauolunca dedio
Io scrissi laltro di alBio prete che me mondasse unaranoleta che era larapera de la nostra
dama delaprofessor nõ mela mondato uiprego uoi hifacriue asapere ụuomo ce p sono che
uenga che io possa sutisoure omaiona che sapere adesso uno anova bisogno altero : ancora
uiprego carissimo Reo che uoi uoliare dire al preto e alasanto che uenendo la traco andor
fioremimo elquale nicuaemo ragionate piu uolte insiemo hiaceme horsou uena dispoeuagno
misimo e uoi ou ou isauite auire e uno amore che certo hiso ublingarissimo quanto che posso
che uiua . Il lararula nõ hohatto pregio enõ lõfino senõ poro p che elsena megno p me che
lanador astima. e pipero pã que ho scritto quello che io nõ poseua e ancora mi uenepasso dane
auuiso pur secondo me oditto epauone de ditto Trupla dice che me dava darune p circha
atrecenti ducati dove p piu enifrancia foro lebesto farsi nescrierre quello che lettuelar morta

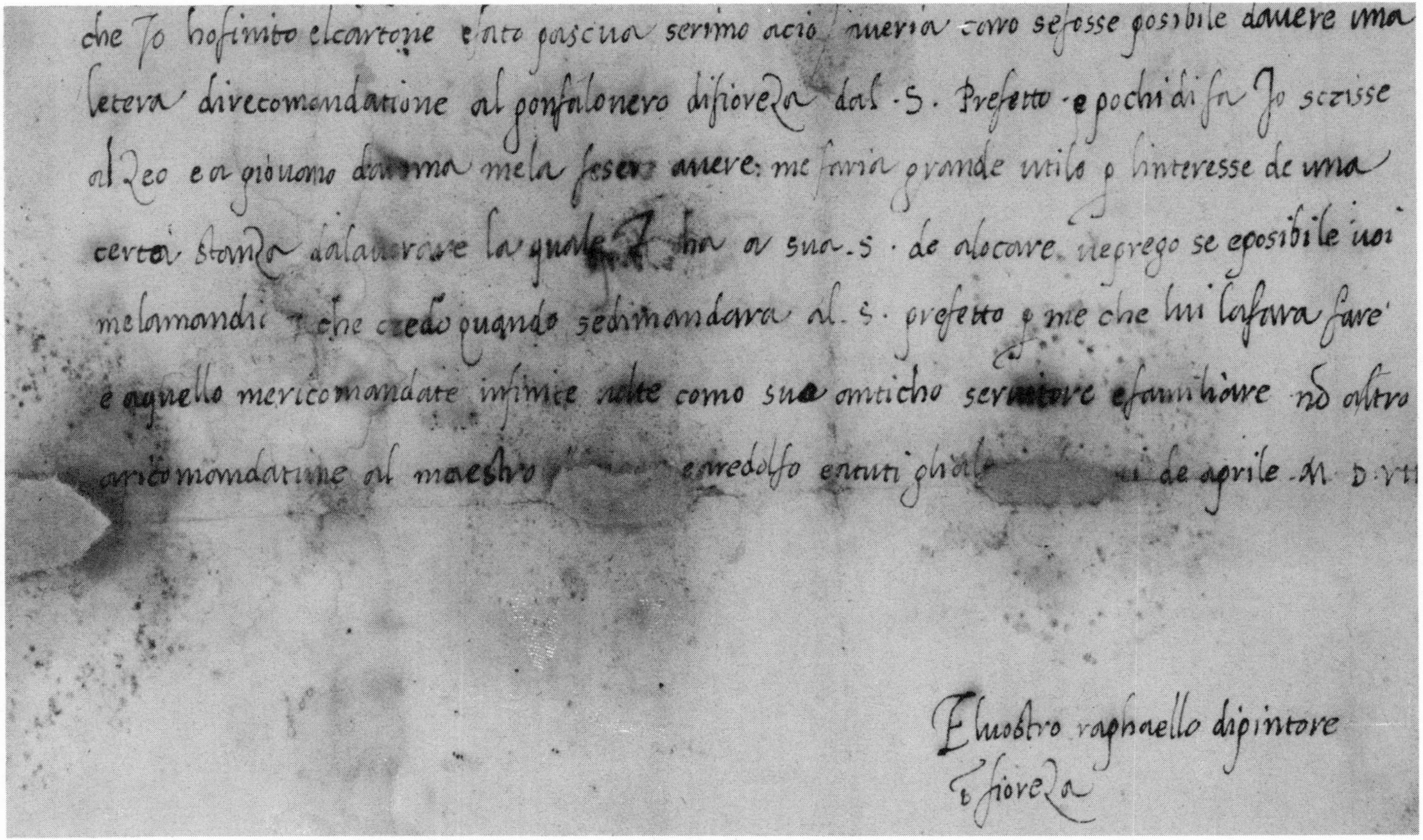

che Jo hofinito elcartone efato pascua seremo acio averia caro se fosse posibile davere una
letera direcomandatione al gonfalonero di fiorenza dal .S. Prefetto e pochi di fa Jo scrisse
al Zeo e a giovanni da roma mela facesero avere: me saria grande utile p linteresse de una
certa stanza dalavorare la quale [illegible] ha a sua .S. de alocare ue prego se eposibile uoi
melamandi [illegible] che credo quando sedimandara al .S. prefetto p me che lui la fara fare
e aquello mericomandate infinite volte como suo anticho servitore efamiliare nō altro
aricomandatime al maestro [illegible] e redolfo e a tuti gli altri [illegible] de aprile .M. D VII[illegible]

El vostro raphaello dipintore
i fiorenza

[2] Letter written by Raphael, April 1508.

P.V·M. GEORGICORVM,
LIBER QV ARTVS.

P
Rotinus aerii mellis, cœlestia dona
Exequar, hanc etiam Mœcenas aspice
partem.
Admiranda tibi leuiŭ spectacula rerŭ,
M agnanimos'q; duces, totius'q; ex ordine gentis
M ores, et studia, et populos, et prælia dicam.
I n tenui labor, at tenuis non gloria, si quem
N umina lena sinunt, audit'q; uocatus Apollo.
P rincipio, sedes apibus, statioq; petenda,
Q uo neq; sit uentis aditus (nam pabula uenti
F erre domum prohibent) neq; oues, hœdiq; petulca
F loribus insultent, aut errans bucula campo
D ecutiat rorem, et surgentes atterat herbas.

[3] Aldus's italic type. 1501.

Among the writing masters of the period, there are three
whose names stand out: Ludovico Degli Arrighi, Giovananto-
nio Tagliente, and Giovanbattista Palatino. All of them produced writing manuals, the first two in 1522 and 1524, the
third in 1540. The examples were cut on wood. Beautiful as

Lutio che'la sua dextra errante' coce',
Horatio sol contra Thoscana tutta',
Che' ne' foco, ne' ferro à virtù noce'.

Johannes Baptista' Palatinus Scribeba'
Romæ, apud Peregrinum
Anno
MDXXXX

[4] Chancery cursive. Palatino's writing manual. 1545.

Saperai anchora Lettor mio che dele littere piccole delo Alphabeto, alcune si ponno ligare con le sue seguenti, et alcune no: Quelle che si ponno ligare con le seguenti, sonno le infrascritte, cioe, a c d f i k l m

[5] Chancery cursive from Arrighi's writing manual.

they are, they have given too many students a false impression of the rhythm of the chancery hand. The flow of the hand is not caught in the plates of these books. This is as much the fault of getting the writing onto the wood blocks as it is the stiffening of forms in the cutting.

In 1523, Arrighi, a papal scribe, published a second manual, also executed in wood blocks. This contained several pages

H æc vates celebrare , sit ter vnus
H ermes , ille opus est , et ipse trinus .
      I dem
D as dotem , et statuas , qui viuus tempore viues
P erpetuo , nequeunt hæc monumenta mori .
H æc igitur Coryti cum sint notissima , notum
N on est , plus dicam te dare an accipere ?
      P . Paulus Thebaldus Ro .

[6] Arrighi. Type from *Coryciana* of Palladius. 1524.

printed from type of his design. The Arrighi type version of the chancery hand was more formal than that of Aldus, simpler and more practical in its avoidance of excessive ligatures. Aldus had adopted the contemporary scribes' style of using small upright roman capitals with a sloping cursive lower case. This practice was followed by Arrighi, but to a modified degree; he used capitals of an intermediate size. Into some of his books, Arrighi introduced decorative, swash italic capitals.

The influence of Aldus Manutius was not solely that of a scholar-printer and typographic innovator. He foresaw the decline of monumental formats in favor of cheaper and more manageable editions. However, he viewed such changes from the vantage point of one who had produced a landmark among the incunabula: the *Hypnerotomachia Poliphili,* containing some of the most influential woodcut illustration and related typography of the Renaissance.

The Woodcut

In the closing years of the fifteenth century, the woodcut reached a new, high level of excellence in the hands of Albrecht Dürer. With his appearance, the independent print takes on added significance in the history of printing. Black and white line is made to carry a richer freight of texture and graphic color. Outstanding craftsmen were required to cut Dürer's designs. Talent attracts talent; it also trains it. I have no doubt that Dürer could have cut anything he drew. In his early teens he had worked with Michael Wohlgemuth, the illustrator of many of Koberger's books. After extensive travel, including an extremely valuable visit to Italy, Dürer returned to a uniquely productive life in Nuremberg. Because he bridged the Gothic and humanistic traditions, Dürer is harder to catalogue than Mantegna, the Italian he admired so much. Vasari recalls Raphael's appraisal that given an acquaintance with the antique, Dürer would have surpassed them all.

This little introduction to Dürer seeks chiefly to provide one bracket for a short exposition of the technique of woodcut-

[7] Dürer. Detail from the *Apocalypse*. 1498.

ting. The closing bracket will be provided by two lesser-known works of Jan Lievens, Rembrandt's friend, and fellow pupil of Pieter Lastman. The period encompassed by the Dürer *Apocalypse* of 1498 and the Lievens portrait woodcuts could be as much as a century and a half. It covers the work of, among others, Hans Holbein, Jost Amman, Lucas Cranach, Hans Baldung (called Hans Grien), Christopher Jegher for Rubens, Nicolò Boldrini for Titian, and Ugo da Carpi for Raphael and others.

Tools and Preparation

A woodcut is made on the plank, that is, a lengthwise section of the tree, rather than on a cross section. In both the East and the West, fruitwoods have been favored. In Japan, the wood has been cherry, and in Europe pear. The chief tool has been the knife, held upright in the East and like a pencil in the West. Auxiliary tools are gouges and chisels, for clearing the spaces between and around the lines of the design.

The drawing may be made directly on the block of wood,

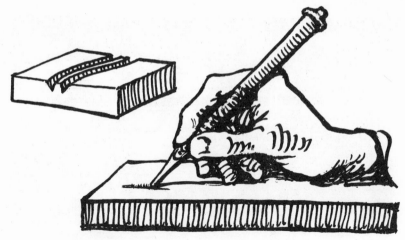

[8] Woodcutting. Position of knife. Diagram of cut line.

or transferred from paper by rubbing the back of a tracing made in soft lead or any similar material. It was once common practice to paste the drawing onto the block, but, like the direct drawing on wood, the original was sacrificed in the cutting.

After the design is satisfactorily prepared, a light tint is usually rubbed over the block. A good transparent blue works well for this purpose. Freshly cut passages thus will show up clearly and to advantage. The positions of the knife, Oriental and Occidental, can best be described in a simple diagram:

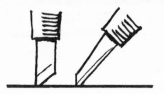

[9] Positions of knives: Oriental and Occidental.

Technique of Woodcutting

The shape of the knife to be used is determined by the angle of cutting, the governing factor being the amount of metal to be drawn through the block. Obviously, the minimum amount is most desirable.

If a curved line is to be cut, its outside rim can be done with relative ease. The block is rotated, usually on a sand-filled leather pad, rather than the hand-turned. The power and control of the woodcutter's stroke are thus increased. An inside curve demands greater care in the cutting, because the back of the knife blade is constantly in danger of injuring the wood as it follows the edge of the design in the cutting.

A first incision is made, along the line, at a 20- to 30-degree angle off the vertical. After the block is revolved half a turn, a second incision, to remove wood adjacent to the line, is made at an angle of 40 to 60 degrees. At this angle, a larger surface section can be removed.

The wood remaining in the spaces between the lines is removed with gouges and chisels. Gouges work best when they are sharpened so that the sides of the *u* or *v* form of the tool are

[10] Gouge for woodcutting.

in advance of its belly. Such sharpening makes possible an action similar to two knives at work, and enables the woodcutter to move easily against and across, as well as with, the grain. Repairing broken or rejected lines is an important capability of the woodcutter, and this he does by trimming and gluing in a fresh piece of wood, then refinishing it. This patch may be so shaped that it is locked into the block, thus being doubly strengthened.

An example of a masterly job of repairing can be seen in the two states shown here of small head by Rembrandt cut by Jan Lievens. The recutting of the mouth required re-establishment of that surface area and represent, to me, the height of the woodcutter's craft. I also discover in them a fundamental com-

[11] Two states of a Rembrandt drawing cut on wood by Jan Lievens.

[12] *Diogenes*, by Parmigianino. Chiaroscuro woodcut by Ugo da Carpi.

A Short History of the Printed Word

[13] *The Cardinal*. Woodcut by Jan Lievens.

ment on the nature of art and craftsmanship: the fact that
Lievens could cut a drawing by Rembrandt gave him invaluable objectivity in cutting works of his own design.

The sixteenth century saw the introduction of chiaroscuro
prints, multiple blocks printed together to give a painterly,
grisaille, or tonally sculptural effect. The simple technique was
to make a key block; this carried the design. The second block
provided a tone for the whole, and into this lights were cut to
relieve and model the forms. A more subtle method is shown in

CHAPTER V · *The Sixteenth Century*   95

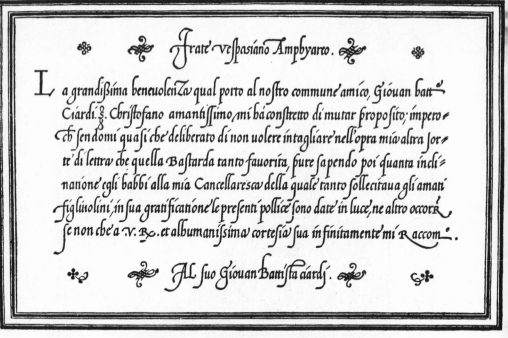

[14] A page from the writing manual of Vespasiano
     Amphiareo. 1554.

Ugo da Carpi's *Diogenes*, cut after Parmigianino's drawing. In
Da Carpi's approach, the key block becomes the accent of the
design, but it is incomplete and would not stand alone.

Works on Letter Forms

Mention of Arrighi, Tagliente, and Palatino should be
accompanied by some remarks on the several important works
about letter design printed at nearly the same time. In Venice,
in 1509, Luca Pacioli's *De Divinia Proportione* appeared. Dürer
produced his *Underweysung der Messung* in 1525 and Tory
produced *Champfleury* in 1529. These three books were attempts to rationalize the proportions of letters and to construct
master patterns. Perhaps the most valuable messages from Pacioli, Dürer, and Tory are to be found in their attitudes toward
the letter forms and their interest in them; they help us to
understand sixteenth-century taste. They make, when coupled
with the writing books of the period, an impressive and perhaps

A Short History of the Printed Word

[15] Cresci. Roman upper and lower case from *Il Perfetto Scrittore*.

unique display of the attention which letter forms were given between 1509 and 1540.

It has been assumed that Ludovico degli Arrighi died in Rome in 1527. His second type face was acquired by Antonio Blado, a printer with an Aldus connection, who became papal printer in 1545 and retained that post until 1567. Thus Arrighi's influence survived him directly for forty years. Blado produced work of great distinction and made a notable contribution in using single and compound florets and arabesque ornaments. In 1556 he published *Il Perfetto Scrittore*, by Giovanni Francesco Cresci, one of the great classic books on letter forms.

The French Masters

After her meager contribution to the first half century of printing, France gradually began to provide the chief centers of influence on the shaping of books. Among those who were to

L.Feneſtellæ de
MAGISTRATIBVS,SACERdotiiſ(q̃ Romanorum libellus , iam primum
nitori ſuo reſtitutus.

Pomponij Læti itidem de magiſtratibus &
ſacerdotijs, & præterea de diuerſis legibus Romanorum.

TEM   PVS.

VIRT VS.SOL A·ACIEM
RETVNDIT·ISTAM

PARISIIS
Ex officina Simonis Colinæi.
1 5 3 9.

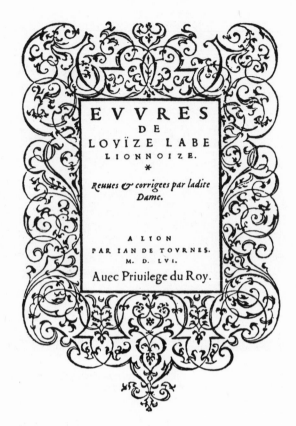

EVVRES
DE
LOYÏZE LABE
LIONNOIZE.
*
Reuues ᶜ corrigees par ladite
Dame.

A LION
PAR IAN DE TOVRNES.
M. D. LVI.
Auec Priuilege du Roy.

[16] Simon de Colines. Title page. 1539.
[17] Jean de Tournes. Title page. 1556.

dominate the printing of the sixteenth century were the Estiennes (Henri and Robert), Simon de Colines, Geofroy Tory,
Claude Garamond, and Jean de Tournes.

The printing dynasty of the Estiennes was founded in 1501
by Henri. In the beginning, he used gothic type, but he turned
to roman, probably under the influence of Aldus. It did not
take long for a type character which was definitely French to
begin to assert itself. The enthusiasm of King Francis I for the
works of the Italian Renaissance gave great impetus to printing
in France. The King lured some of the greatest artists and
craftsmen away from Italy, including Andrea del Sarto and
Leonardo da Vinci.

DE TRANSITV
Hellenifmi ad Chrifti-
anifmum, Lib.primus.

ONSIDERANTI MI-
hi fæpenumero, Frácifce rex po-
tétiffime, ad eámque mentis inté
tioné veheméter incúbéti, quod-
nam dignum operæpreciū ex vfu
philologiæ, atque è literarum cō
fuetudine ferre poffem: & verò
fcire auenti quo pacto potiffimū
meliorē hominis interioris con-
ditione, ex eo labore ftudióq; efficerē, cui externa & corporis bona quæ dicta funt, pofthabéda, ætate quoque flo-
rentiffima duxeram:cupiditas inceffit adeundæ tandem &
confulédæ philofophiæ. Philofophia autē (inquit apud
Platonem Socrates in Phædone)mortis eft meditatio, eò
demum ipfa fpectans, vt anima corpori nunc cōfociata,
hinc tandem fublimis abeat,corporifque contagione de-
functa morte facili, ad deum creatorē fuum rapiatur, cu-
ius illa fimilitudine ab eodem ipfo prædita eft, quàm fie-
ri poteft integerrima ab ipfius corporis focietate. & quidem ipfius philofophiæ munus eft, id quod homines no-
runt difcendi cupidiffimi, animam vt hominis docēdam
fufcipiat,corpori alligatam,atque illi conglutinatam, &
verò neceffariò coactam, quafi per carcerem quendam, fic

A.i.

[18] Robert Estienne. Chapter opening. Initial by Tory.

Geofroy Tory

Among those who had worked for Henri Estienne, as a
reader, was a many-sided genius named Geofroy Tory, who
was born about 1480 in Bruges and died in 1533. He was
at various times a lecturer in philosophy, publisher's reader,
bookseller, typographer, engraver, and printer. In orthogra-
phy, he introduced the apostrophe, accents, and cedilla to
printing. After study in Italy, he carried his version of the
Aldine style into France. En route, it became Tory's own, and
proved to be the most influential typographic force in Europe.
Tory lightened the color of roman and the color of the woodcut decorations, initials, and illustrations which complemented
it. An example of his decorative approach is shown in the
Horae of 1525. In 1529, Tory produced his famous *Champ-*

Ad fextam Verfus.

Eus in adiutorium meũ intende.
R.Domine ad adiuuandũ me fe
ſtina. Gloria patri, & filio,& ſpi
ritui ſanĉto. Sicut erat in princi
pio,& nunc,& ſemper, & in ſecu
la ſecuſorum. Amen. Alleluia.   Hymnus.

[19] Geofroy Tory. *Horae.* 1525.

fleury, a major work on letter design. The following year he
was named *Imprimeur du roi.*

Claude Garamond, one of the most famous type designers
of all printing history, was one of the artist-craftsmen who were
attracted to the Tory circle. Garamond was born in 1480, but
as with so many key figures in typographic history, his life is
not well documented. As a youth, he began cutting punches.
This indicates that he probably worked on gothic fonts before
he came under Tory's influence. Although there are no proofs

A Short History of the Printed Word

[20] Estienne's *Cicero*, with type by Garamond.

or books to show such an early direction, it is reasonable to assume that he worked for numerous printers, perhaps with Simon de Colines as well as Robert Estienne. It is known that with the latter acting as adviser, Garamond cut his *Grec du Roi*, a cursive based on the handwriting of Angelos Vergetios, the King's "écrivain en grec." The punches for this type, completed around 1541, were cut in three sizes. Between 1540 and 1545, Garamond cut the several sizes of his roman and italic. The type made its first appearance in *Ciceronis Opera*, printed by Robert Estienne in the years 1543–4. From that time on, the romans and italics of Garamond and his followers were a staple in typographic inventories.

Much has been made of the model Garamond used, especially his freedom from dependence on calligraphic forms. My reaction to this is twofold. First, printed books had become accepted to a degree where it was no longer necessary, or even

Non erat forma ei, neque decor.

[21] Type by Garamond, from a showing of his *canon* size.

199

DIONYSII HALICARNASSEI 33
PRÆCEPTA DE ORATIONE PANEGYRICA,
M. Antonio Antimacho interprete.

20

Anegyris, solennis scilicet quinquennalium ludorum celebritas siue côuentus, est inuentum & donum deorum, ad requiem maiorum rerum quæ ad vitam attinent, tradita (sicuti quodam in loco inquit Plato) cum dii humanum genus ad laborem natum miserati essent. Coacti autem fuerunt a sapientissimis hominibus conuentus, & a ciuitatibus publice communi decreto, ad reficiendos recreandosq; animos, ac ad oblectationem atque solatium spectantium constituti. Tributus vero ad hos mutuo celebrandos, est a diuitibus suppeditandarum quidem pecuniarum sumptus, a principibus circa hoc ornatus ad magnificentiam apparatus, rerumq; ad id commodarum opulentia. Panegyrim athletæ corporum robore ornant plurimum; & Musarum ac Apollinis assectatores musica, quæ in ipsis reperitur. At virum, qui in litterarum & eloquentiæ studiis versatus fuerit, ac vniuersum vitæ tempus in eis consumpserit atq; contriuerit, in ornanda panegyri ita sese gerere oportet, ac tanto inniti artificio, vti eius oratio a vulgari dicendi ratione abhorreat. Age igitur, o Echecrates, ad hoc tamquam duces viæ nequaquam tritæ nec a multis tentatæ facti, explicemus tibi ea quæ olim a nostratis sapientiæ parentibus nobis tradita accepimus:illi vero, & illorum etiam superiores, a Mercurio & a Musis habuisse dixerunt: non secus ac Ascrɛus pastor ab eisdem in Helicone poesim est consecutus. Age itaq;, cum huiusmodi arte orationes sequere.Deus etenim vniuersɛ,quæcumq; sit, panegyrios aliquo modo præses, & eiusdem est nominis: vt, Olympiorum, Olympius Iupiter: eius autem quod in Pythiis fit certaminis, Apollo. Principium igitur huiusmodi orationis,quæcumq; fuerit,laus dei nobis sit, tamquam vultus seu persona quædam splendida, in sermonis initio posita atque constituta. Laudandi autem exordium, ab iis quæ deo insunt, eique attribuuntur,prout res copiam suppeditant,sumes.Si quidem Iupiter fuerit, adducendum erit, deorum regem, rerumque omnium opificem esse : Si vero Apollo,musices inuɛtorem exstitisse,& eundem esse cum sole: Solem autem omnium omnibus bonorum auctorem. Præterea si Hercules erit, Iouis esse filium: & ea quæ mortalium vitæ præbuit, cônumerabis.Et locus ferme côplebitur ex ijs quæ quilibet aut inuenerit, aut hominibus tradiderit. Verum hæc breuibus narrabis; ne præcedens oratio sequenti maior euadere videatur. Deinceps vrbis laudes,in qua publicus conuentus celebratur,vel a situ,

30

40

r ij

[22] Garamond type printed in Frankfurt by Wechel.

desirable, to make them resemble manuscripts. Second, and more important, it was inevitable that type would respond to the working qualities of steel, just as written alphabets had responded to the qualities of the quill and the reed. The essential fact in all successful types has been the translation of the model into metal, and not the mere imitation of the characteristics of a pen. Aside from the highly satisfactory shapes which Garamond gave to his romans and italics, he made a basic contribution in bringing the two forms into a working relationship. He also developed larger italic capitals to use with his italic lower case.

A career of such industry and talent would seem to guarantee worldly success, but with Garamond this was not the case. He died in poverty in 1561. He was eighty-one years old and had been living on at "Pot Casse," the house that Tory had occupied. His widow sold his punches and mats, and some of these eventually reached printers whose fame was to match Garamond's: Le Bé, Fournier, and Plantin.

Basel: Johann Froben, Hans Holbein, and Others

During the first quarter of the sixteenth century, a distinguished collaboration developed in Basel. Johann Froben, the printer, had as his scholar-editor Erasmus, and as his illustrator-decorator the young Hans Holbein. Froben was one of the most renowned publishers of humanist literature, and in the pre-Tory days managed to exert significant influence on European printing, including that of Paris and Lyons. Holbein's *Dance of Death* was printed in Lyons by the Trechsel brothers in 1538, but the blocks were cut in Basel.

Among the important books printed in Basel was Froben's own New Testament in Greek, with a Latin translation by Erasmus. It appeared in 1516. From the printing office of Michael Isengrim, also of Basel, a large botanical work by Leonhard Fuchs was issued in 1543; its title was *De Historia Stirpium*. Drawings of the plants, by Fullmaurer and Meyer, were cut on wood by Rudolff Speckle.

An outstanding work on anatomy was brought out by Oporinus in 1568. The author was Andreas Vesalius and the title *De Humani Corporis Fabrica*. The illustrations by Jan

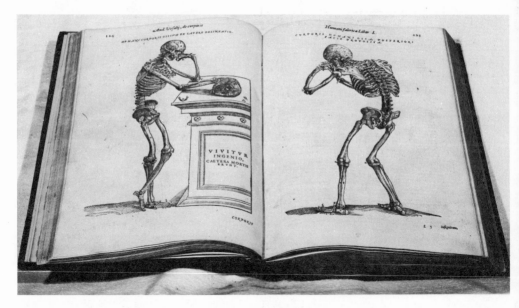

[23] Vesalius. *De Humani Corporis Fabrica*. 1553.

Stevenszoon Van Calcar are still accepted as classic examples of anatomical drawing and are used in several manuals for artists.

The Tory Influence in France

The influence of Basel in the middle of the sixteenth century began to be overshadowed by the more elegant, lighter, and more Latinate style developing in France under the leadership of Tory. The achievements of Jean de Tournes and Christophe Plantin at this time were outstanding. De Tournes was born in 1504. He worked with the Trechsels, became foreman of the printing office of Sebastian Gryphius, the first printer of Rabelais, and in 1540 opened a shop of his own. De Tournes worked at Lyons, and over some two dozen years gained a reputation for scholarship and excellence of design that placed him among the greatest of French printers. He was known for his arabesque woodcut borders, which in time were turned into type ornament by his punch-cutter. Some of these elements of De Tournes are still available in the stock ornaments of modern printers. A fine example of his arabesque is the title page of Louise Labé's *Evvres*. Another excellent example of his style is

A Short History of the Printed Word

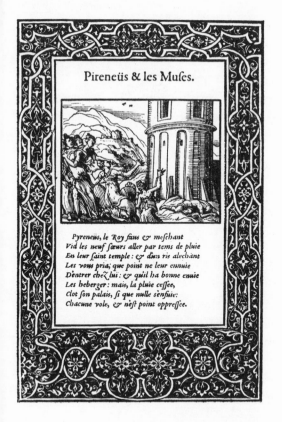

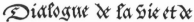

[24] Jean de Tournes. *Métamorphose d'Ovide.*
[25] Robert Granjon. Title page using *civilité*. 1557.

the *Métamorphose d'Ovide Figurée* with woodcut illustrations
by Bernard Salomon.

A strong link connecting De Tournes in Lyons and Plantin
in Antwerp was Robert Granjon, the able French punch-cutter
who worked for both men. Granjon was a Parisian with experience in all the phases of early typography: publishing, printing,
punch-cutting, and type founding. His name is especially associated with a type called *civilité* (because it had been used in *La
Civilité Puérile* by Erasmus) that was based on French Gothic
cursive handwriting. The italic used in the Ovid is by Granjon.
His connection in Lyons with Gryphius and De Tournes introduced him to Bernard Salomon, the designer-illustrator,
whose daughter Antoinette he married.

Antwerp: Christophe Plantin

Plantin was in many ways the antithesis of De Tournes. While De Tournes was an artist with a dedicated sense of purpose, Plantin was, in the main, a businessman with a keen sense of publishing. Plantin, who was born in France about 1520, made his reputation in Antwerp, where the Plantin-Moretus Museum stands in our time as a major public monument to a printer. Plantin established a bindery in Antwerp in 1549, and six years later added printing and publishing to his undertakings. He continued his work until his death in 1589, and was succeeded by his widow and his son-in-law, Jan Moretus.

Plantin's talent seemed to lie in the size of editions, rather than their typographic excellence, and he might be described as one of the earliest practitioners of merchandising. He made books with a look of opulence, profusely illustrated and utilizing artists and designers more for their names than for their understanding of the basic nature of letterpress printing.

Between 1568 and 1572 the printing office of Plantin was engaged in a large undertaking commissioned by Philip II of Spain; an eight-volume publication whose title was *Biblia Regia*. Printed in five languages—Hebrew, Greek, Aramaic, Latin, and Syriac—it was known as the Polyglot Bible. The edition consisted of 13 sets for the King, on vellum, and 1200 on paper for general sale. It was a very large undertaking indeed, considering the capacity of the presses available.

Plantin is famous for his generous use of copper engravings. Even as early as the Polyglot Bible, some of the illustrations were engraved. In 1559, the Plantin shop had done the letterpress text for a commemorative book marking the death of Charles V. The illustrations for this were designed, and probably printed, by Jérôme Cock, Pieter Brueghel's father-in-law. Use of engraved or etched intaglio prints necessitates an additional impression, with a different type of press. Despite the added cost of production, copper began to supplant wood, and Plantin and his descendants led the way.

Antwerp was better supplied with engravers than most centers. A leading figure in the field of engraved prints was Jérôme Cock, who engraved the large body of work designed by Brueghel. When Rubens's studio was in full operation, it em-

REGNI NEAPOLITANI
PRIVILEGIVM.

PHILIPPVS DEI GRATIA REX
CASTELLÆ, ARAGONVM, VTRIVSQVE
SICILIÆ, HIERVSALEM, VNGARIÆ, DALMATIÆ, ET CROATIÆ, &c.

NTONIVS Perrenotus, S.R.C.tit. Sancti Petri ad Vincula Presbyter, Cardinalis de Granuela;præfatæ Regiæ & Catholicæ Maieftatis à confiliis ftatus, & in hoc Regno locum tenens, & Capitaneus generalis, &c. Mag.co viro Chriftophoro Plantino, ciui Antuerpienfi, & præfatæ Catholicæ Maieftatis Prototypographo fideli Regio, dilecto, gratiam Regiam & bonam voluntatem. Cùm ex præclarorum virorum literis certiores facti fimus, opus Bibliorum quinque linguarum, cum tribus Apparatuum tomis, celeberrimum, reique publicæ Chriftianæ vtiliffimũ, eiufdem fereniffimæ Maieftatis iuffu, ope atque aufpiciis, ad publicam totius Chriftiani orbis commoditatem & ornamentum, typis longè elegantiffimis, & præftantiffimi viri Benedicti Ariæ Montani præcipua cura & ftudio. quàm emendatiffimè à te excufum effe, eiufdemq́; exemplar fanctiffimo Domino noftro PP.Gregorio XIII. oblatum, ita placuiffe, vt præfatæ Maieftatis fanctos conatus, & Regi Catholico in primis conuenientes, fummopere laudarit, & ampliffima tibi priuilegia ad hoc opus tuendum Motu proprio concefferit; Nos quoque cum naturali genio impellimur ad fouendum præclara quæque ingenia, quæ infigni quopiam conatu ad publica commoda promouenda atque augenda afpirant; primùm quidem longè præclariffimum hoc fuæ Maieftatis ftudium, vt verè Heroicum & Ptolomęi, Eumenis, aliorumque olim conatibus in Bibliothecis inftruendis eò præftantius, quòd non vanæ ftimulo gloriæ, vt illi, fed rectæ Religionis conferuandæ & propagandæ zelo fufceptum, meritò fufpicientes; deinde eximiam operam doctiffimi B. Ariæ Montani, ac immortali laude dignam admirantes, rebusque tuis, quemadmodũ tuo nomine expetitur, profpicere cupientes, ne meritis frauderis fructibus tantæ operæ, & impenfæ, quæ fumma folicitudine & induftria in opus ad finem feliciter perducendum à te etiam infumpta effe accepimus; cumque certò conftet, opus hoc nunquam hactenus hoc in Regno excufum effe, dignumque ipfo S. fedis Apoftolicæ fuffragio fit iudicatum vt diuulgetur ac priuilegiis ornetur. Tuis igitur iuftiffimis votis, vt deliberato confilio, ita alacri & exporrecta fronte lubenter annuentes; tenore præfentium ex gratia fpeciali, præfatæ Maieftatis nomine, cum deliberatione & affiftentia Regij collateralis confilij, ftatuimus & decreuimus, ne quis intra viginti annos proximos, a die dat. præfentium deinceps numerandos, in hoc Regno dictum Bibliorum opus, cum Apparatuum tomis coniunctis, vel Apparatus ipfos, aut eorũ partem aliquam feorfum, citra ipfius Chriftophori, aut caufam & ius ab ipfo habentis, licentiam imprimere, aut ab aliis impreffa vendere, aut in fuis officinis vel aliàs tenere poffit. Volentes & decernêtes expreffè,
quòd

[26] Christophe Plantin. Polyglot Bible. 1572.

ployed a group of engravers especially trained to translate his paintings into prints. Balthazar Moretus, grandson of Plantin and a friend of Rubens, brought the great Flemish painter into several collaborations with the Plantin shop. The first of these was a commission to illustrate a *Breviarium Romanum* in the seventeenth century.

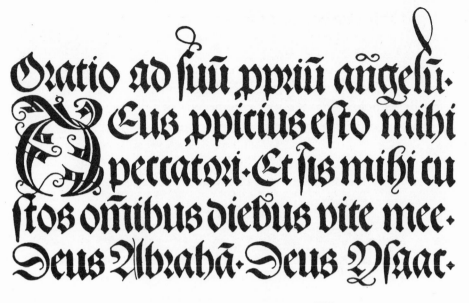

[27] Johann Schoensperger. *Fraktur*. 1514.

Textur and Roman in Germany and England

During the period when Tory and Garamond were contributing to the design of roman and italic types, certain ameliorations were taking place in the German *lettre de forme*. The
Textur of Gutenberg's time began to develop in two directions
—the pointed gothic, called *Fraktur*, used in the prayer book of
the Emperor Maximilian I, printed by Johann Schoensperger in
1513—and a rounder, more cursive black letter, with *bâtarde*
characteristics, that became known as *Schwabacher*. The dictionary calls *Schwabacherschrift* "German italics."

Despite the widespread use of *Fraktur* in Germany, Garamond's roman and Greek types were in the hands of Andreas
Wechel and Konrad Berner at Frankfurt and they continued to
be used there. The influence of Jacob Sabon, the punch-cutter
from Lyons, began to be felt when, in 1571, he married the
granddaughter of Christian Egenolff and operated Germany's
first independent type foundry. In 1572 John Day introduced
roman type into England. It marked the beginning of the disappearance of gothic forms from English books.

A Short History of the Printed Word

Hie hat ein ende das lesen esopi⸗
Die vorrede Romuli philosophi in das buͤch Esopi⸗

Romulus seinem sun von der stat athenis heýl⸗Eso
pus ist gewesen ein simreýcher man auß kriechen
der durch sein fabeln die menschē gelert hat⸗wie sý
sich in allem thůn vnd lassen halten soͤllen⸗Aber darumb das
er das leben der menschen vnd auch jre sitten erzeýgen moͤ

[28] Johann Schoensperger. Modified *Schwabacher*. 1491.

The Seed of Stereotyping

Two technical achievements of 1568 and 1569, both in the field of map-making, had wide meaning and application. The first advance marked the publication of a map of Bavaria. Although the map was cut on wood, which was common practice, the identifying place names were set in type, made into mats, and cast in lead. The castings were cemented into the wood blocks in a technique that foreshadowed stereotyping, the process whereby newspapers make the castings from which they print. The second achievement was the publication of Mercator's world map for mariners, which was engraved on twenty-four large copper plates.

CHAPTER V · *The Sixteenth Century*   109

The sixteenth was a French century and, although in its latter years no new Estiennes or De Tournes had appeared, the year 1580 saw the first publication, in Bordeaux, of a great work of the French spirit: *Essays*, by Michel de Montaigne. Although there had been no significant typographical developments in England, her turn was due. In 1558, Elizabeth became Queen. In 1593 and 1594, Shakespeare published his first works, *Venus and Adonis* and *The Rape of Lucrece*. The century closed on a note of great promise for creative literature.

ESS*A*yS

DE MICHEL

DE MONTAI-
GNE.

LIVRE SECOND.

A BOVRDEAVS.
Par S. Millanges Imprimeur ordinaire du Roy.
M.D.LXXX.
AVEC PRIVILEGE DV ROY.

[29] Montaigne's *Essays*. Title page. 1580.

CHAPTER VI

The Seventeenth Century

JOHN MILTON, addressing Parliament in 1643, spoke out for freedom of the press and against an act that required that all books, pamphlets, and papers be licensed by an official censor before publication. The full text was published in November 1644 and was titled *Areopagitica*, from the speech by Isocrates to the Great Council of Athens, the Areopagus.

I deny not, but that it is of greatest concernment in the Church and Commonwealth, to have a vigilant eye how books demean themselves, as well as men; and thereafter to confine, imprison, and do sharpest justice on them as malefactors. For books are not absolutely dead things, but do contain a potency of life in them to be active as that soul whose progeny they are; nay, they do preserve as in a vial the purest efficacy and extraction of that living intellect that bred them. I know they are as lively, and as vigorously productive, as those fabulous dragon's teeth; and being sown up and down, may chance to spring up armed men. And yet, on the other hand, unless wariness be used, as good almost kill a man as kill a good book; who kills a man kills a reasonable creature, God's image; but he who destroys a good book, kills reason itself, kills the image of God, as it were in the eye. Many a man lives a burden to the earth; but a good book is the previous life-blood of a master-spirit, embalmed and treasured up on purpose to a life beyond life. 'Tis true, no age can restore a life, whereof perhaps there is no great loss; and revolutions of ages do not oft recover the loss of a rejected truth, for the want of which whole nations fare the worse. We should be wary therefore what persecution we raise against the living la-

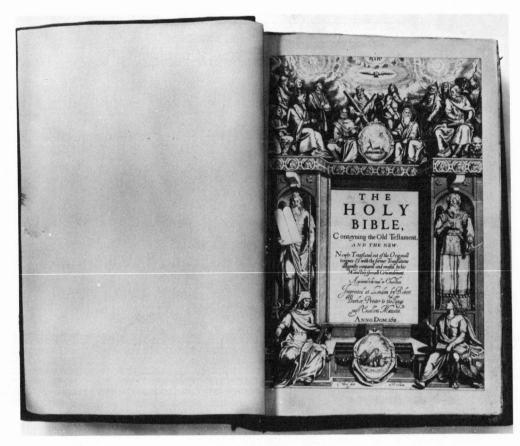

[1] The King James Bible. 1611.

bours of public men, how we spill that seasoned life of man pre-
served and stored up in books; since we see a kind of homicide
may be thus committed, sometimes a martyrdom, and if it ex-
tend to the whole impression, a kind of massacre, whereof the
execution ends not in the slaying of an elemental life, but strikes
at that ethereal and fifth essence, the breath of reason itself, slays
an immortality rather than a life. . . .

Censorship in England

In 1637 the number of print shops and foundries in England had been limited by decree. In the cradle years of printing,
opposition came chiefly from organized calligraphers and illuminators whose livelihood was threatened. The content of

A Short History of the Printed Word

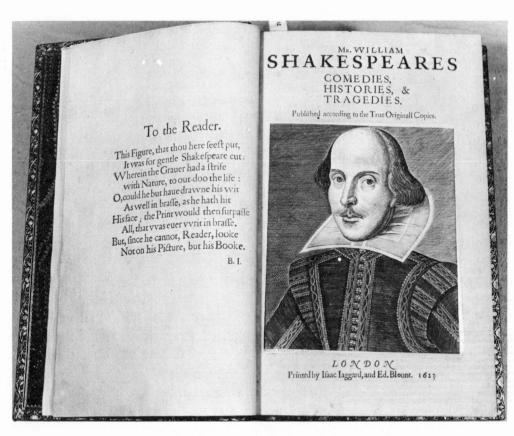

To the Reader.

This Figure, that thou here seest put,
It was for gentle Shakespeare cut;
Wherein the Grauer had a strife
with Nature, to out-doo the life :
O, could he but haue drawne his wit
As well in brasse, as he hath hit
His face ; the Print would then surpasse
All, that vvas euer vvrit in brasse.
But, since he cannot, Reader, looke
Not on his Picture, but his Booke.

B. I.

Mr. WILLIAM
SHAKESPEARES
COMEDIES,
HISTORIES, &
TRAGEDIES.
Published according to the True Originall Copies.

LONDON
Printed by Isaac Iaggard, and Ed. Blount. 1623.

[2] Shakespeare. First Folio. 1623.

manuscripts was seldom in question; most were classics or ecclesiastical writings and many were in Greek or Latin, which
made them inaccessible to all but a few scholars and churchmen.
But with the coming of the seventeenth century, printing was
being viewed as a threat to established power, both religious
and political. The opposition took the form of censorship. Milton's words did not bear immediate fruit; however, Parliament's Declaration of Rights of 1689, which preceded the
proclamation of William and Mary as King and Queen, fore-
told his triumph. In 1694 the Licensing Act expired. It was not
renewed, and censorship of the press ended.

In the seventeenth century, printing was introduced in
eight countries: the Philippines, 1602; Lebanon, 1610; Bolivia,
1610; America, 1639; Iran, 1640; Finland, 1642; Norway,
1643; and, in Western form, China, 1644.

CHAPTER VI · *The Seventeenth Century*   113

The Bible, Shakespeare, and Cervantes

In England, in addition to laws and decrees that threatened the press, there were great upheavals and natural disasters. From 1642 to 1646, the Civil War between the Royalists and the Parliamentarians divided the country. In 1665 and 1666,

A
DECREE
OF
Starre-Chamber,
CONCERNING
PRINTING,

Made the eleuenth day of July last past. 1 6 3 7.

¶. Imprinted at London by *Robert Barker*,
Printer to the Kings moſt Excellent
Maieſtie: And by the Aſſignes
of *Iohn Bill.* 1 6 3 7.

[3] Star Chamber decree. Title page. 1637.

the Plague and the Great Fire struck London. It is possible that government restrictions on printers and foundries were more effective in limiting technical advances in England than were war, plague and fire. The genius of the country, however, had never shown itself in fine printing and outstanding presswork, but in great writing. In the first quarter of the seventeenth

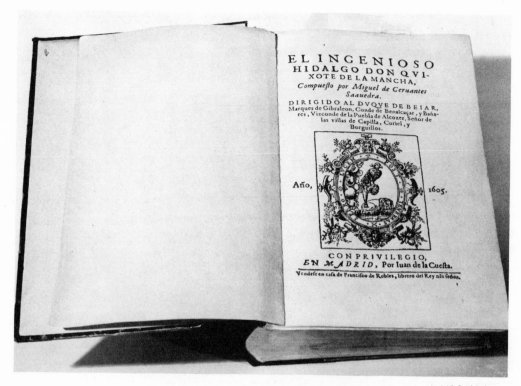

[4] Cervantes. *Don Quixote.* 1605.

century, the two most often printed books in the English language appeared: the King James Version of the Bible, and the First Folio of the Shakespeare plays.

The Bible translation had been ordered by James I in 1604, the year after he was proclaimed King. Forty-seven translators were engaged in the task. The book appeared in 1611, and the printer was Robert Barker, who also printed *A Decree of Starre-Chamber Concerning Printing*, in 1637, the decree limiting printing and type founding.

A third major literary event during the first quarter of the century was the publication in Madrid in 1605 of *El Ingenioso Hidalgo Don Quixote de la Mancha*, by Miguel de Cervantes. The title page shows the pervasive French influence in establishing the character of roman types being used in Europe after Tory and Garamond.

[5] Engraved illustration by Rubens for *Pompa Introitus Ferdinandi.* 1641.

Plantin and the Elzevirs

In describing the work of Christophe Plantin, the publisher-printer of Antwerp, we noted that Peter Paul Rubens designed illustrations and decorations for the Plantin house for a number of years. In 1614 he illustrated *Breviarium Romanum*, and his last work for the Plantins was *Pompa Introitus Ferdinandi*, issued in 1641, after Rubens's death. Engravings after Rubens's designs show both the virtues and the shortcomings of the medium. It provided great range and color for such a talent as his, but the result was not an integral part of the typography of the book he was decorating. I believe the designs would have been better served if they had been cut on wood by Rubens's woodcutter Christopher Jegher, who executed the *Temptation*

[6] Rubens. *Temptation of Christ*. Woodcut by Jegher.

of Christ. One reason this was not done was that the Plantin establishment was committed to the use of engravings.

As a kind of footnote on Rubens and the printers, there is an indication from his friend Balthazar Moretus, Plantin's grandson, that the great painter demanded much time and money. Rubens himself gave some clue to his evaluation of the importance of work he did for the Plantins by restricting it to Sundays, as if it were a hobby.

In a more modest way, the duodecimo (sections of 12 leaves or 24 pages) books of the Elzevirs, with their engraved title pages, were produced, using much the same merchandising approach as the Plantins. (Today, designers of trade books are often faced with the attitude, on the part of publishers, that the jacket is more important than the text, resulting in more attention being given to the former than to the latter.)

The Elzevirs rivaled the Plantins for commercial longevity and Aldus for dedication to the small format. Louis Elzevir, founder of the enterprise, was born about 1542. His business,

[7] Elzevir. *Republica*. 1627.

begun in 1583, was engaged in publishing only. It was not until 1618 that the Elzevir family bought presses. Their small-format editions that were to become so popular and widely imitated were begun in 1629, when Bonaventure Elzevir and his nephew, Abraham, controlled the firm. The type face they used was by Christoffel van Dijck, a goldsmith of Amsterdam, who was one of the greatest of the seventeenth-century Dutch type founders. He was the teacher of Anton Janson and the designer of some of the types acquired for the presses of Oxford and Cambridge Universities. After his death, his foundry was bought by the Elzevirs.

The Oxford University Press was established in 1667, and for it, in 1672, Bishop John Fell purchased Dutch punches and mats for the fonts known as the Fell types. The punches had been cut by Dirk and Bartholomew Voskens. Along with the Van Dijck faces previously purchased for Oxford, the Voskens

ABCDEFGHIKLMNOPQR
STVUWXYZ ABCDEFGHIK-

PAter noster qui es in cœlis, san-
ctificetur nomen tuum. Veniat
regnum tuum: fiat voluntas tua,sicut
in cœlo, ita etiam in terra. Panem nostrum quotidianum da nobis hodie.

AABCDEFGHIJKLMM
NOPQRSTVUWXYZÆÆ

PAter noster qui es in cœlis, sanctifi-
cetur nomen tuum. Veniat regnum
tuum: fiat voluntas tua, sicut in cœlo, ita
etiam in terra. Panem nostrum quotidia-
num da nobis hodie. Et remitte nobis de-

[8] The Fell types, roman and italic.

fonts account for much of the seventeenth-century Dutch influence on English type founding.

Intaglio

In many sixteenth-century books, and especially in the publications of the Plantin-Moretus shop in Antwerp, the illustrations were engraved on copper plates and printed *intaglio*. The
popularity of engraving increased, and use of the medium expanded in response. Many great seventeenth-century painters
and draftsmen made designs for the engravers and etchers of
the time, and some executed their own plates. Unfortunately,
there are too few examples from the most gifted, but the list is

impressive: Rubens, Rembrandt, Van Dyck, Goltzius, Poussin, Callot, De Hooge, Hollar, and De Passe.

The influence of the intaglio method on printing goes far beyond its employment by etchers and engravers. It foreshadowed in its original uses the eventual development of rotogravure, a printing method that was to allow the use of a fine screen in the fast and inexpensive production of magazines and newspapers.

Intaglio, as used in the engraving sense, describes any printmaking process by which ink is transferred to paper from areas below the surface. Ink is forced into the engraved lines, or tones, and then the surface of the plate is wiped clean. The press is so constructed that it delivers a rolling pressure similar to the action of a clothes wringer. The paper has to be driven into the lines to lift out the ink. The press consists of a bed that travels between two steel rollers. A felt blanket, between the upper roller and the paper and plate on the bed, acts as the make-ready, a self-adjusting overlay.

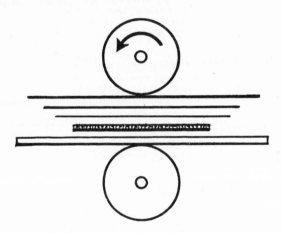

[9] Pressure system for intaglio printing.

Engraving

An engraving consists of lines made with a shaped, forged, and finished steel tool, sharpened at the end and set into a handle that allows thrust to be given through the palm of the hand rather than through the fingers.

The engraver's plate is held against a leather, sand-filled pad, which allows the work to be turned into the stroke and provides sufficient friction to keep it from sliding. Values of lines may be varied both in their width and depth. Unlike letterpress, intaglio printing can have ink deposits of different depths. A beautiful example of an engraved plate, translated

[10] Title page by Poussin. Engraved by Mellan. 1642.

[11] Etched illustrations by Rembrandt. 1655.

from a drawing, is the title page of Horace's *Opera* by Nicolas Poussin. It was engraved by the distinguished French portrait engraver Claude Mellan.

Etching

The intaglio method used by Rembrandt was etching. He carried it to extraordinary heights. The principal etching tools are a steel needle, pointed and pencil-like in size, a scraper and burnisher to erase and polish the surface of the plate, acid-resisting *ground*—consisting of wax, mastic, and asphaltum or amber—a grounding roller, and stopping-out varnish. The plate, of copper, zinc, or steel, must be evenly heated before the acid-resisting ground can be rolled on. The surface of the plate is smoked with lampblack, using a wax taper, to provide a background against which the bright metal shows as the needle draws through the wax.

A Short History of the Printed Word

[12] Rembrandt. Etching made as a line cut to show how
his style might have worked for letterpress.

There are several ways to execute a design for etching.
First, the drawing can be carried forward during the various
stages of the etching process, so that the lightest portions are
drawn in last, and consequently are least exposed to acid. Second, the design can be drawn in its entirety, then the plate put
in the acid bath for its initial biting. When the lightest lines
have sufficient depth, the plate is removed and the light section
painted over with stopping-out varnish. The plate is put in the
acid bath again, and the next lightest lines determine the timing.
This is continued until the design is completely bitten, or
etched.

The etchings by Rembrandt, made in 1655 as illustrations
for *La Piedra Gloriosa o de la Estatua de Nebuchadnesar* by
Samuel Menasseh ben Israel, examples of his late style, are
among his few published illustrations.

CHAPTER VI · *The Seventeenth Century*

[13] Aquatint by Goya.

Aquatint and Mezzotint

The tonal effects in engraving and etching are dependent on the proximity of the lines to each other, on the weight of the lines, and to some extent on manipulation in the inking process. The intaglio methods inherently tonal are aquatint and mezzotint.

Aquatint is a form of etching in which resin is floated onto the plate by means of a solvent, or is dusted onto the plate, which is then heated to cause the grains of resin to adhere. With brush and stopping-out varnish, the sections of the design that are to be light in tone are painted in. The plate is put in the acid bath, and the less light sections are bitten. This process is repeated, as in regular etching, until only the darkest portions are left for the final biting. The resin ground allows the acid to attack the plate in uniformly separated spots, which appear on

A Short History of the Printed Word

the final print as slightly irregular but relatively uniform black dots. Their size and closeness depend on the length of time they have been etched. It is possible to combine an etched line with the use of aquatint. This was Goya's method.

In 1641, Ludwig von Siegen invented mezzotint, a technique that so worked the plate with serrated metal rollers (roulettes) and tooth-studded rockers that the surface metal was upset, or roughened. Thus roughened, it would hold ink and print in tones, the values of which depended on the closeness and depth of the roughnesses. Once the surface of the plate had been prepared to hold ink, it could be worked back with scrapers and burnishers, to whatever degree of lightness was required. To achieve longer printing runs, steel was often used

[14] Mezzotint by Doughty after Reynolds.

instead of copper for intaglio printing. Mezzotint became a favored method for reproducing portraits. An example is Doughty's mezzotint of Dr. Johnson, made from the Joshua Reynolds portrait.

Intaglio printing is a completely different concept of impression from relief printing. The two methods are not compatible and must be printed separately. Engraving requires

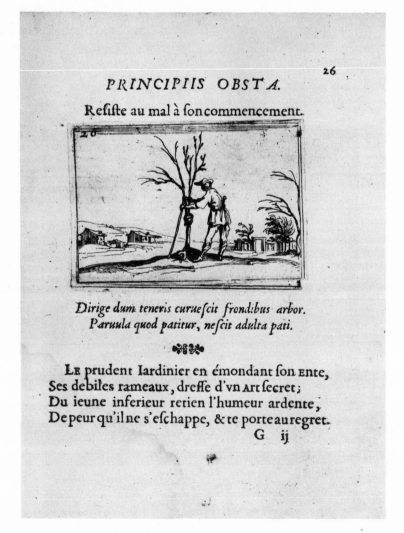

[15] Callot. Illustration for *Lux Claustri*. 1646.

stiffer inks and greater pressures than relief. The fact that the entire plate acts as a bearing surface makes for a delicacy of lines that is the hallmark of engraving. But this virtue can be compromised by the difficulty of removing the ink completely and cleanly from the surface of the plate.

Perhaps the most influential as well as prolific of the seventeenth-century illustrators was Jacques Callot, a French engraver and etcher whose early training was received in Italy. Callot is credited with developing the hard varnish ground and with instituting the practice of successive biting. While most of his prints were sold independently or as collections of etchings with engraved titles or captions, he did several books with illustrations in intaglio, the text being printed by letterpress. Such a volume is his *Lux Claustri* of 1646. Callot's simple and open style appears to return to the typographically inspired woodcut illustrations of the late fifteenth and early sixteenth centuries for its sources. The tendency of most artists and craftsmen had been the opposite: woodcutting, as it survived, had attempted to imitate engraving.

The First Newspapers

A landmark in seventeenth-century printing history was the publication by Johan Carolus of Strasbourg, in 1609, of the world's first newspaper: *Avisa Relation oder Zeitung*. Earlier efforts in this line had taken the form of single sheets devoted to special events and had appeared irregularly, as occasions warranted. England's first news publication of substance was issued the year before the First Folio, in 1622, by Nathaniel Butter, Nicholas Bourne, and Thomas Archer.

As the seventeenth century was a time of strict censorship in England, John Archer's first *coranto*, of 1621, landed him in jail. Holland, after successfully expelling the Spanish at the beginning of the century, became an independent state and was a haven in Europe for journalists. Because of its maritime position, the country also enjoyed unusual opportunities for gathering news. The birth of the Dutch press is dated 1618, when the

[16] *Avisa Relation oder Zeitung*. The first newspaper. 1609.

Courante Uyt Italien, Duytslandt began to appear regularly. It continued as a weekly for forty years.

After 1620, the Thirty Years' War caused an expansion of news sheets from single pages printed on both sides to issues as large as eight pages. As Holland became a political refuge, it served as headquarters for the clandestine press that penetrated the neighboring states where news was rigidly controlled. Industrial prosperity, increased literacy, and a phenomenal period of distinction in the arts and in scholarship were reflected in the growth of the Dutch press. In 1656 the *Weckelycke Courant van Europa* was started. It is Holland's oldest newspaper, still surviving as *Nieuwe Haarlemsche Courant*.

France, as well as England, was served by the clandestine news sheets produced in Holland. There was an annual publication, *Mercure de France*, as early as 1605, and a weekly, *Nouvelles Ordinaires de Divers Endroits*, was begun in 1631.

[17] John Archer's *Coranto* of 1621.

The former was taken over by Cardinal Richelieu after he became adviser to Marie de Médicis. The latter, after a lifespan of five months, was superseded by the *Gazette*, published by the King's doctor under a special privilege granted by Richelieu. The *Gazette* continued for more than 150 years as the official source of news and comment.

Although Germany had the first newspaper of regular publication, the *Avisa Relation oder Zeitung* of 1609, and Frankfurt had its first weekly in 1615, her power-jealous rulers preferred to allow Dutch papers into their domains rather than permit a native free press. A common pattern appears in the means of suppression—royal decree, censorship by law, licensing both to restrict and to grant the right of publication, and, not least, repressive taxation.

The fact that the first English-language news sheets appeared in Holland may be taken as evidence of the state of

CHAPTER VI · *The Seventeenth Century* 129

[18] The first English-language news sheet. 1620.

English censorship in 1620 with its application of Star Chamber ordinances and royal patents to restrict the size and the performance of the press. In 1625, Charles I expressed his royal will by dissolving Parliament and suppressing all news sheets. This included the efforts of Thomas Archer and his collaborators, Nicholas Bourne and Nathaniel Butter. Following strong protest, Butter and Bourne were rewarded in 1638 with the sole right to print news in their revived *coranto*.

After the proclamation of the commonwealth, Cromwell promulgated anti-press measures as repressive as those of the kings who preceded him. With the restoration of the monarchy, Charles II put a royalist cavalry officer, Roger L'Estrange, in charge of licensing, and the result was L'Estrange's own *Publick Intelligencer* of 1663. Henry Muddiman, who was to have shared the right to print news, was kept from doing so by his rival, the King's licenser. But the great London plague of 1665

A Short History of the Printed Word

[19] *The London Gazette*. 1665.

caused the court to be moved to Oxford, and there the King, lacking printed news, allowed Muddiman to begin a single sheet, semi-weekly paper. It was printed on both sides and was called the *Oxford Gazette*. When the court returned to London, the *Oxford Gazette* went with it, becoming and remaining the *London Gazette*.

Newspapers in the American Colonies

The climate of censorship was little different in England's American colonies than in the mother country. It was too easy to lose one's equipment, let alone be fined and imprisoned, for many to risk the displeasure of royal governors.

One means of news dissemination in the colonies was the correspondence of merchants and leaders with their friends both abroad and in the colonies. In some instances, correspond-

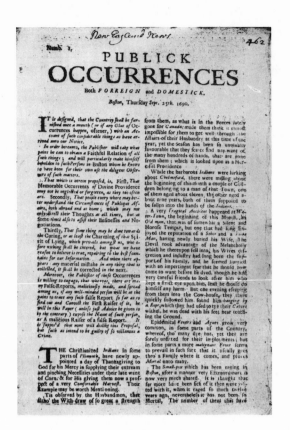

[20] Harris's *Publick Occurrences*. 1690.

ence was carried on by professional letter-writers, set up in various world centers. A second means of communication existed in the importation of packets of newspapers for the customers of coffeehouses and taverns, long accepted as centers of news distribution and the informal conduct of business. The official *London Gazette* was especially favored for such American circulation. In several instances, issues of the *Gazette* were reprinted in the colonies.

The first American newspaper was not attempted until September 1690, when *Publick Occurrences Both Forreign and Domestick* was published in Boston by Benjamin Harris. Four days after its appearance the governor and council of the colony declared the paper to have been issued without authority, and thus ended its life after a single issue. It was small in format, 6 inches by 9½ inches when folded, and was composed of four

A Short History of the Printed Word

pages. The third was left blank in case the purchaser wished to write in a news bulletin before passing it on.

The Imprimerie Royale

The seventeenth century was a period of magnificent literary achievement: it was the time of Shakespeare, Cervantes, and Milton, of Molière, Corneille, Racine, Donne, Bunyan, and Dryden. Despite such literary genius, the most luxurious editions of books were institutional publications, especially those of the state. The books of the Imprimerie Royale are a good example.

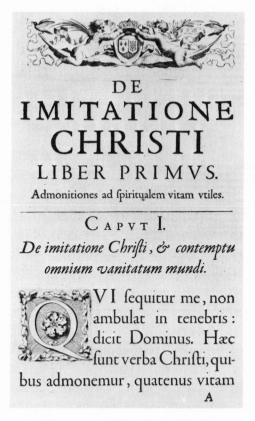

[21] Opening chapter of the first publication of the Typographia Regia.

The Imprimerie Royale, known also as the Typographia Regia was established in 1639–40 for Louis XIII at the suggestion of Cardinal Richelieu. Its first publication was *De Imitatione Christi*, completed in 1642, a folio volume set in types based on Garamond. For the second publication, a work by the Cardinal himself was chosen, and the type was Jean Jannon's *caractères de l'Université*. This face was credited to Garamond until 1926.

Romain du Roi Louis XIV

Types of the Imprimerie were reserved to its use only, under stiff penalties. The first director appointed by Richelieu was Sebastien Cramoisy; he was followed by his grandson Sebastien Mabre-Cramoisy. When the latter died, and his successor, Jean Anisson, was named in 1691, it was proposed that a new type face be cut for the Typographia Regia. This proposition was turned over to a group of academicians, headed by a mathematician named Nicolas Jaugeon. Their solution was to construct an alphabet on the basis of cross-sectioned, equi-sided rectangles, each containing 2,304 squares. The master designs for this alphabet were engraved by Simonneau, but the task of cutting the punches was given to Philippe Grandjean, who fortunately was able to follow his own instincts as well as the patterns of the academicians. The result was a transitional letter, known as the *romain du roi Louis XIV*. The first publication using the new type was an imposing *Médailles sur les Événements du Règne de Louis-le-Grand*, in 1702.

The patterns that Grandjean was asked to use provide an excellent example of the kind of influence engraving was exerting on all aspects of typography and illustration. The pictorial and decorative influences have been discussed. In Simonneau's plates, the letters were rendered from indications made on cross-sectioned paper by academicians rather than by calligraphers. Jaugeon's alphabet was, from its beginning, a rationalized, not an esthetic, concept. The graver was not able to function as a sculptural tool, and the results suffer greatly by comparison with the efforts of Dürer, Pacioli, Cresci, Tory, and others. Their letter-forms were based on the influences of chisel and flat pen.

[22] A plate by Simonneau for Jaugeon's *Romain du roi*.

The most widely accepted writing books of the seventeenth century were engraved. Van de Velde's *Thresor Literaire*, Rotterdam, 1605, and Pisani's *Tratteggiato da Penna*, Genoa,

135

[23] Page from Pisani's *Tratteggiato da Penna*. 1640.

1640, are examples. The pen work in both books is flamboyant and excessively embellished. It shows the use of a pointed pen responding to pressures that will produce controlled hairlines or swells, and it foreshadows the calligraphy of the coming century. More and more, writing imitated printing.

Presses in the Seventeenth Century

There was little development, meanwhile, in the mechanics of printing. Presses continued to be made of wood. About 1620, Willem Blaeu of Amsterdam improved the connection of the platen and the screw by introducing a spring and suspending the platen. As shown in Joseph Moxon's *Mechanick Exercises*, London, 1683, some presses of the time were equipped with crank-operated traveling carriages. Moxon was an instrument-maker and printer who added type founding to his enterprises in 1659. His type-specimen sheet was the first issued in England, as was his book on the crafts of printing and founding.

A Short History of the Printed Word

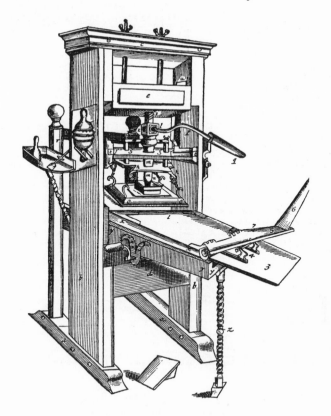

[24] Hand press from Moxon's *Mechanick Exercises*. 1683.

Printing in North America

Seventeenth-century printing has a special meaning for Americans. Late in 1638, Stephen Day set up his press at Cambridge, Massachusetts. He was newly arrived from England, having intended to work as a pressman for the Reverend Jesse Glover, with whom he had sailed. But Glover died and was buried at sea. Day's *Bay Psalm Book* was published in 1640. In 1639, he printed *The Oath of a Free Man*, but no copy of it has survived. The press continued until near the close of the century. After 1649 it was operated by Samuel Green, who, with Marmaduke Johnson, printed the first Indian Bible in 1663. The translation was by John Eliot.

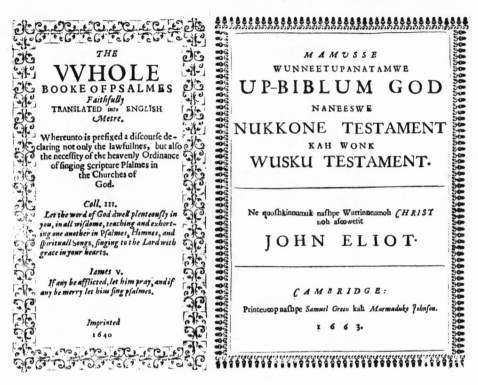

[25] Bay Psalm Book. 1640.
[26] First Indian Bible. 1663.

During the second half of the century, several print shops were established in the American colonies. John Foster set up a press in Boston in 1675, and in 1682 and 1685 printing was introduced in Virginia and Pennsylvania by William Nuthead and William Bradford. Nuthead did not remain long in Virginia; he moved to Maryland in 1686. Bradford continued in Philadelphia, and in 1690 he joined with Mennonite Bishop William Rittinghausen in establishing at nearby Roxborough the first American paper mill. Their partnership was brief, since Bradford had differences with local authorities. In 1693, he moved to New York, where he established the first press in that colony.

Restrictive English laws over printing were reflected in the meager number of presses appearing in the colonies during the half-century following Day's start in Cambridge. Some of the great English cities were also denied licenses. To be a printer was a dangerous calling, and continued to be so even after the relaxed conditions that followed the Declaration of Rights and the subsequent lapsing of the licensing laws. All governments regarded the press as a threat and feared popular involvement in affairs of state. Perhaps the most extreme expression of the ruling point of view was contained in the 1671 report of Virginia's colonial governor, Sir William Berkeley:

But I thank God we have not free schools nor printing; and I hope we shall not have these three hundred years. For learning has brought disobedience and heresy and sects into the world, and printing has divulged them and libels against the government.

The leading news source for the colonists was the *Gazette*, the official London paper that began regular publication in 1665. In 1685, Samuel Green reprinted an issue of the *Gazette*, and more than a decade later a second issue was reprinted in New York by William Bradford. In 1690 Benjamin Harris's *Publick Occurrences Both Forreign and Domestick* aroused the "high resentment" of the Governor and Council of Massachusetts and was suppressed, after its first issue, with a warning to him and all others that it was forbidden for "any person or persons to set forth anything in Print without License first obtained."

A more constructive and forward-looking aspect of state intervention in publishing came when Frederick III, Elector of Brandenburg, ordered that two copies of each book printed within his principality be provided free for deposit in the state's library. The year was 1699. The Elector thus established a reasonable means for the preservation of all the printed works for which he had authority to speak.

The great typographic work in progress at the close of the seventeenth century was the cutting of the *romain du roi* for Louis XIV, and the printing of the sumptuous *Médailles*. As

LE
BOVRGEOIS
GENTILHOMME,
COMEDIE-BALÈT,
FAITE 'A CHAMBORT,
pour le Divertiſſement du Roy,

Par I.B.P. MOLIERE.

Et ſe vend pour l'Autheur
A PARIS,
Chez PIERRE LE MONNIER, au Palais, vis-à-vis
la Porte de l'Egliſe de la Sainte Chapelle,
a l'Image S.Louis, & au Feu Divin.

M. DC. LXXI.
AVEC ·PRIVILEGE DV ROY.

ATHALIE
TRAGEDIE
Tirée de l'Ecriture ſainte.

A PARIS.
Chez DENYS THIERRY, ruë ſaint Jacques,
à la ville de Paris.

M. DC. XCI.
AVEC PRIVILEGE DV ROY.

[27] Title pages for Molière and Racine.

final examples of late seventeenth-century title pages, two are
shown that serve, each of them, a double purpose—the French
style of handling contemporary work, and examples of the
literary genius flourishing at the time. Molière's *Bourgeois
Gentilhomme* was printed in 1671 by Pierre le Monnier. Racine's tragedy, dated twenty years later, was produced by
Denys Thierry. Both were published in Paris.

A Short History of the Printed Word

CHAPTER VII

The Eighteenth Century

PHILIPPE GRANDJEAN's *romain du roi*, which was begun in 1693, was not completed in all its eighty-two fonts until 1745. After Grandjean's death in 1714, the remaining punches were executed by Jean Alexandre and Louis Luce. The first work in which this type was used was the sumptuous folio of 1702, *Médailles sur les Événements du Règne de Louis-le-Grand*. The new face met with swift and wide public approval. To capitalize on the popularity of Grandjean's new style, printers and founders had to skirt the laws decreeing heavy penalties for selling and copying the royal designs. This was first accomplished through a series of ameliorations on existing alphabets.

The influence of the *romain du roi* was evident throughout the eighteenth century and into the nineteenth. It was as much the influence of intaglio engraving as of any set of letters. What is chiefly to be noted is the virtual disappearance of calligraphy as a model for letter forms, and with it the disassociation of formats from the influence of manuscripts.

Grandjean's Romain du Roi

The example, here, is a detail taken from the *Médailles* folio of 1702. A first study shows clarity, mechanical perfection both in form and fitting, and a strong horizontal effect. The latter is a natural result of the insistent use of thin, unbracketed serifs. Such a serif is related to copper engraving rather than to punch-cutting. Especially novel is the continuation of the serifs across the ascending stems and the tops of *i* and *j*. A further unique and identifying touch is the small serif-like extension on

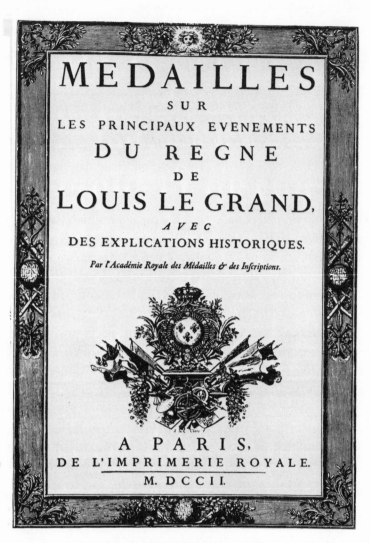

[1] Title page, *Médailles.* 1702.

the lower-case *l*, midway and on the left.

More careful examination of Grandjean's design reveals his basic change of accent from that of Garamond, whose type recalls the romans of Jenson, Aldus, and Tory, with their common ancestry in the pen-written forms of the *scrittura umanistica*. Their thicks and thins fell at an angle to the horizontal. In the *romain du roi* a more mechanical and balanced use of the horizontal occurs. By the end of the eighteenth century, the strong accenting caused by thin serifs and thick-

A Short History of the Printed Word

Enfin il marcha vers Condé, & ayant pris d'abord
cauld, il fit faire un logement fur la contrefcarpe
mefme, 25 d'Aouft, le Gouverneur fe rendit à la fe
Comte demeura aux environs de cette Place jufq
bre, & cette entreprife n'ayant efté faite que pour
ou pour les attirer à un combat, il abandonna Cc
Campagne, & prit Maubeuge en revenant.

CONDATUM ET MALBODIUM CAPTA. M
Condé & de Maubeuge. 1649.

[2] *Romain du roi.* 1702.

ened stems gave an effective decorative quality to a page of
such type, but at great cost to legibility. Roman has come to be
divided into three categories. Those having calligraphic stress
and bracketed serifs are *old style. Romain du roi* was the forerunner of the types called *transitional.* The third category,
modern, is applied to those alphabets, starting with Bodoni's
in 1790, which have lost all relationship to written models.

Old style
Transitional
Modern

[3] Examples of old style, transitional, and modern types:
Caslon, Baskerville, and Bodoni.

Louis Luce, the last of the three punch-cutters to work on
the *romain du roi,* made his own attempt to produce a font that
would have novelty and appeal to the taste of his time, yet in no
way be imitative of the restricted designs of the Imprimerie
Royale. Over some thirty years, beginning in 1740, he cut the
first condensed roman in France. For it, he claimed qualities of

delicacy and simplification as well as special practical advantages in the setting of poetry. Luce called his type face the *Poétiques*. However, his plan to produce a letter for public use was cut short in 1744, when Louis XV ordered that the royal press purchase all the fonts and the decorations that went with them. There, the ornaments saw more use than the type.

William Caslon

It has been apparent in almost all the examinations of English printing and founding that neither art was highly developed in England during the first two and a half centuries after Gutenberg. Nor were they even modestly influential. Since the English had produced fine manuscripts and through Alcuin of York had shared in the development of the all-important Carolingian script, such a sterile record is hard to account for. The climate of the seventeenth century provided some explanations

Quoufque tandem abutêre, Catilina, patientia noftra ? quamdiu nos etiam furor ifte tuus eludet? quem ad finem fefe effrenata jactabit audacia ? nihilne te nocturnum præfidium palatii, nihil urbis vigiliæ, nihil timor populi, nihil con-
ABCDEFGHIJKLMNOPQRS

Quoufque tandem abutére, Catilina, patientia noftra ? quamdiu nos etiam furor ifte tuus eludet ? quem ad finem fefe effrenata jactabit audacia ? nihilne te nocturnum præfidium palatii, nihil urbis vigiliæ, nihil timor populi, nihil con-
ABCDEFGHIJKLMNOPQR

[4] Caslon *Old Face* (*Great Primer*). 1734.

—civil war and harsh government regulation. In the eighteenth century, the style and production of British presses and founders began to develop national characteristics that became generally influential.

The chief influence on English printing had been Dutch, and it was strengthened when William Caslon, the most successful and celebrated of English type founders, chose Dutch models for his famous *Old Face*. Caslon was born in Worcestershire in 1692, and was apprenticed to a gun engraver in London. In 1716, he set up his own shop for decorating guns and he added work in silver-chasing and in cutting binders' dies. Among the few English type manufactories operating in the early seventeenth century was the James foundry; it was there that Caslon is presumed to have been taken to observe the rudiments of punch-cutting and casting.

A decorator of gun locks and barrels would have invaluable knowledge about working with steel. In addition to his experience with the necessary tools, he would have been required to make small punches for striking names and dates into lockplates. Familiarity with the sculptural techniques of counter-punching would provide an attitude toward punch-cutting that was more closely related to that of earlier centuries than to Caslon's own. Grandjean and Luce used counter-punches, but they thought in terms of gravers.

Caslon's first type was an Arabic font for use by the Society for Promoting Christian Knowledge. From that time, about 1720, to the issuing of his first specimen sheet in 1734, Caslon produced numerous fonts, among them Hebrew, Coptic, and black letter, in addition to his range of roman and italic.

Upon the first Caslon's death in 1766, William Caslon II succeeded to the leadership of the foundry. The family's control continued through three quarters of the nineteenth century. Since the Caslon face was produced and introduced in America during the final decades of colonial government, it occupies a special place in American typography.

A contemporary comment, accompanying a 1738 reprint of Caslon's specimen sheet, referred to him as one who,

TANDEM aliquando, Quirites! L. Catilinam furentem audacia, ſcelus anhelantem, peſtem patriæ nefarie molientem, vobis atque huic urbi ferrum flam-
A B C D E F G H I J K L M N O P.

TANDEM aliquando, Quirites! L. Catilinam furentem audacia, ſcelus anhelantem, peſtem patriæ nefarie molientem, vobis atque huic urbi ferrum flammamque minitan-
A B C D E F G H I J K L M N O P Q R.

[5] Baskerville roman (*Great Primer*). 1762.

"though not bred to the art of letter-founding, has, by dint of genius, arrived at an excellency in it unknown hitherto in England." It has often happened that an amateur has made more impression on a period of English printing than the whole collection of professionals. William Caslon had too much experience with steel to put him into the class of amateur type designer. A better example is the second most influential English type designer, John Baskerville.

John Baskerville

He was born in 1706 and his first work was as a writing master in Birmingham. Next he became a successful maker of japanware—articles varnished and decorated in the Japanese manner. He was forty-four years old when he became interested in various aspects of typography and established a foundry, printshop, and paper mill. In style, Baskerville's letters belong to the group called transitional. One of his special contributions was the development of hot-pressed papers. Using a dampened *wove sheet*—made on a woven screen rather than the usual chain and laid style—he subjected it to pressure between hot copper plates after its impression. The silky finish of

PUBLII VIRGILII

MARONIS

BUCOLICA,

GEORGICA,

E T

AENEIS.

BIRMINGHAMIAE:

Typis JOHANNIS BASKERVILLE.

MDCCLVII.

[6] Title page for Baskerville's *Virgil.* 1762.

the Baskerville pages, the brilliance of the specially formulated ink, and the severe, undecorated typography won high praise in Europe. In time, the effect that Baskerville achieved with hot plates was built into papers by calendering, or pressing between rollers before printing.

The three characteristics expected of a writing-master-turned-tray-and-snuffbox-painter would be neatness, an interest in letters and their general arrangement, and a strong dedication to finish. All these factors go into John Baskerville's contribution to founding and printing. His presswork is especially notable and represents perhaps his greatest contribution. In 1762, the year of his *Virgil,* he issued a specimen sheet from which examples are taken.

147

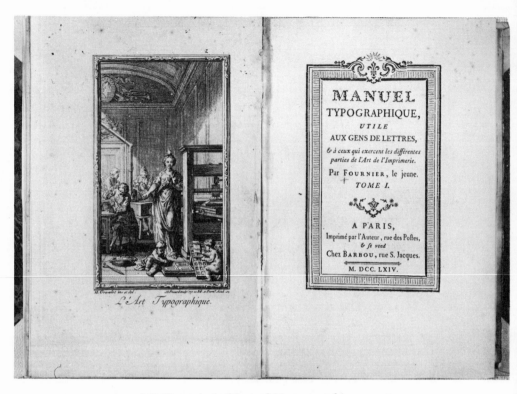

[7] Fournier's *Manuel Typographique*. 1764.

The Fourniers

In France, in the 1760's, Luce was working on his condensed typeface, the *Poétiques*. At the same time, Madame de Pompadour was engaged in printing Corneille with the help of a group of professional printers ordered in by the King from the Imprimerie Royale. Two distinguished printing families were also at work in France, the Fourniers and the Didots. Both are famous for their contributions in establishing more orderly means of typographic measurements. In 1764 Pierre Simon Fournier published his *Manuel Typographique*, the first part of which covered the subjects of type and type-founding. He included, under founding, an exposition of his "point system," which had been formulated as early as 1737 and had been described in some detail in his *Modèles des Caractères* of 1742. By the time the *Manuel* appeared his plan had been somewhat simplified. In essence, Fournier had established a scale which he divided into 2 inches. The inch was further divided into 12 lines. Each line was made up of 6 typographic points.

ÉCHELLE FIXE

de 144 points Typographiques.

[8] Fournier's scale.

In addition to descriptions and tables, Fournier provided a series of plates illustrating the tools used in the processes described.

In his second volume of the *Manuel,* Fournier discussed sizes and styles of types, showed fonts from numerous European sources, and gave accounts of the foundries themselves. Some of the examples were furnished by Jean Pierre Fournier l'aîné, the oldest of the brothers. Fournier l'aîné purchased, in 1730, the famous Le Bé foundry, which had been managed by his father, and thus fell heir to some of the great surviving punches and mats by Garamond, Le Bé, Granjon, and San-lecque. He was an engraver and founder, but he never received the attention given his younger brother, Pierre Simon.

Fournier le jeune was born in Paris in 1712. He was given some private art training and was connected with the Académie de Saint Luc. His brother's foundry provided the opportunity

IL eſt vrai, Monſieur, que le chagrin a pɪ chez moi, & qu'il ne faut pas moins que de ſouvenir que vous me donnez, pour mè d

Id genus eſt hominum peſſimum ,
In denegando modò queis pudor eſt pa

[9] Fournier le jeune type printed by Didot. 1743.

149

for him to work as a wood-block cutter and to begin his training as a punch-cutter. In 1742, Pierre Simon issued a specimen book, which he titled *Modèles des Caractères de l'Imprimerie et des Autres Choses Nécessaires au Dit Art*. It contained, in addition to examples of type including initial letters, an impressive display of decorative material. The printing was done by Jean Joseph Barbou, whose shop dated from the sixteenth century. Joseph Gérard Barbou, a nephew, was responsible for printing all of the books of Fournier le jeune, except his *Modèles*.

The Didots

The Didot family began in Paris in 1713 with François Didot, a bookseller and printer who numbered among his authors the Abbé Prévost. An example of his typography is the title page of his edition of *Les Aventures de Télémaque*, by Fénelon. Various members of the Didot family have been engaged in founding, printing, and paper-making, often making outstanding contributions, during succeeding generations. It is the son of François, François Ambroise, and the grandsons, Pierre l'aîné and Firmin, who require a place in the story of French printing of the eighteenth century.

François Ambroise Didot was a type founder and printer. In addition to the patronage he received as printer-by-appointment to the brother of Louis XV, he was commissioned by the King himself to produce a series of French classics. In 1785, Benjamin Franklin arranged with François Ambroise to have his grandson, Benjamin Franklin Bache, learn the art of punch-cutting at the Fournier foundry.

Didot was responsible for introducing to France the smooth and highly finished paper known as wove, similar to the one developed by Baskerville. However, Didot's name is chiefly associated with the European point system by which type is measured. He recognized certain basic shortcomings in the Fournier system. For one thing, the scale, especially as printed in the *Manuel* on dampened paper, was subject to shrinkage,

LES AVENTURES

DE TÉLÉMAQUE,

FILS D'ULYSSE.

PAR M. DE FÉNÉLON.

IMPRIMÉ PAR ORDRE DU ROI

POUR L'ÉDUCATION

DE MONSEIGNEUR LE DAUPHIN.

A PARIS,

DE L'IMPRIMERIE DE FRANÇ. AMBR. DIDOT L'AINÉ.

M. DCC. LXXXIII.

[10] Title page by F. A. Didot. 1783.

PROSPECTUS.

des Peintures antiques de PIETRO-SANTE
ns une seconde édition au public, parut p
Paris, en 1757. Deux illustres savants, le C
te, consacrerent les plus grands soins à l'e
si intéressante, afin qu'elle répondît à la ce

[11] Type used by F. A. Didot. 1782.

151

ODE I.

AD VENEREM.

INTERMISSA, Venus, diu

ˑsus bella moves. Parce, precor,]

Non sum qualis eram bonɛ

[12] Type used by Pierre Didot. 1799.

which could make it inaccurate. And even a metal prototype Fournier had designed lacked a standard of comparison. Didot's contribution was to adopt the French *pied au roi* as his standard, with 12 French inches, each of which would contain 72 points. Thus the Fournier point concept was retained. (The metric system was not established in France until 1799.) Didot also introduced the present style of identifying type sizes by their point body measure rather than by the traditional names, such as parisienne, nonpareil, petit-romain, cicéro, gros-texte, and gros-romain.

The two sons of François Ambroise Didot, Pierre l'aîné and Firmin, carried on the work of the printing plant and the type foundry. Pierre l'aîné was permitted to use the space in the Louvre that had been occupied by the Imprimerie Royale, and there he printed and published his éditions du Louvre. The younger brother, Firmin, continued his father's direction in type-founding and further developed the style now associated with the name. The Didots were deeply involved in the approaching Neo-classicism, and like their contemporary, Bodoni, represent the coming nineteenth century, which witnessed the flowering of their styles.

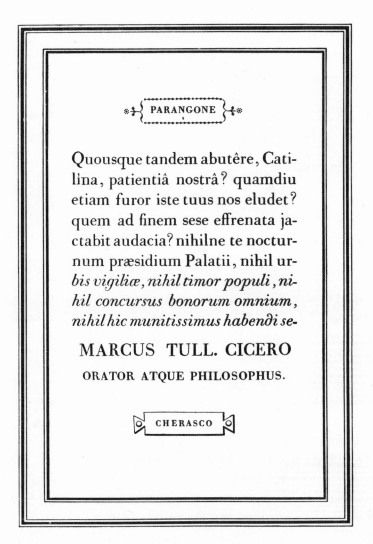

Quousque tandem abutêre, Catilina, patientiâ nostrâ? quamdiu etiam furor iste tuus nos eludet? quem ad finem sese effrenata jactabit audacia? nihilne te nocturnum præsidium Palatii, nihil urbis vigiliæ, nihil timor populi, nihil concursus bonorum omnium, nihil hic munitissimus habendi se-

MARCUS TULL. CICERO

ORATOR ATQUE PHILOSOPHUS.

CHERASCO

[13] Bodoni. Specimen.

Giambattista Bodoni

Giambattista Bodoni was born in Italy in 1740. He was the son of a printer and served his apprenticeship in Rome, where he began experimenting with type-cutting. He wanted to go to England to work but was thwarted by an illness during his journey. When he was twenty-eight years old, he was invited to take charge of the *Stamperia Reale*, which belonged to the Duke of Parma. His stock of types came from Fournier in

[14] Bodoni. *Manuale Tipografico.*

Paris, and some of the punches he cut at that time reveal the influence of Fournier.

In 1790, Bodoni was asked by the Spanish Minister to the Papal Court to direct the printing of a series of classics. This offer resulted in a better arrangement with the Duke of Parma, with regard to both equipment and time. As printer to Carlos III of Spain, and as printer for Walpole and other English authors, Bodoni enjoyed the kind of fame that is possible only when there is a conjunction of opportunities that are realized and exploited.

The Enschedés

Many of the most impressive works of the eighteenth century, from the *Médailles* of the Imprimerie Royale of 1702 to Bodoni's *Manuale Tipografico,* represent great technical advances: better casting and fitting of the types, paper with more consistent printing surfaces, and better ink and presswork. Printing took on the look of engraving to an astonishing degree. The tendency had begun with the Grandjean serifs for the *romain du roi* and it came to full expression in the accentuated thicks and thins favored by Bodoni and Firmin Didot.

In 1743 the brothers Isaak and Johannes Enschedé bought the facilities of an Amsterdam type founder named Heinrich Wetstein and removed them to Haarlem, where they operated a printing plant. This plant, which became one of the most famous in Europe, continues to function, and through acquisition and conservation can claim one of the largest collections of antique punches and mats in the world. The Enschedés' most favored type-cutter during the eighteenth century was Johann Michael Fleischman, a German born in Nuremberg who was working in Geneva when he sold his first types to the parent foundry of the Enschedés. Fleischman was called "a very clever type-cutter" by Fournier. I know that he was greatly admired by Rudolf Koch. It is possible that Koch felt some kinship with Fleischman because they were born in the same city, but, chiefly, he was aware of their common sculptural attitudes toward punch-cutting.

Working with the Enschedé foundry, although set up independently, was François Rosart (1714–70). He never became reconciled to the Fleischman ascendancy and finally left Haarlem to return to his native Belgium. He is remembered for his early experiments in developing type for music printing. In this his name is linked with the more successful Johann Gottlieb Immanuel Breitkopf (1719–94) of Leipzig. In 1754, Breitkopf perfected the system whereby each element of notation was a completely independent unit of type. Fournier knew Breitkopf, and called his foundry the most interesting of any he knew in Germany.

Printing in Spain

Works by Joaquín Ibarra, Gabriel de Sancha, Francisco Manuel de Mena—all of Madrid—and Benito Montfort of Valencia represent the best of eighteenth-century Spanish printing. The interest of Carlos III in printing was shown when he gave Bodoni his special patronage. In addition, the King en-

[15] Breitkopf. Title page. 1784.

Parvula ne scopulis pereat fallacibus Argo:
Non aliter baculo cautus rimare sagaci
Stagnantis vada cæca viæ, luteasque paludes
Sedulus explora, sitne alto in gurgite fundus,
Ne temerè instabili credas vestigia limo,
Ne cedente solo, tacitâque repentè ruinâ
Tibia, sura, genu tumulentur mersa barathro.

[16] Type used for *Obras Sueltas.*

couraged printing in his own country, especially in those cities where the craft had once been practiced.

Ibarra's celebrated "Academy Edition" of *Don Quixote,* a quarto (sections of 4 leaves or 8 pages) in four volumes, was

[1] Numb. 1.

A

Weekly Review

OF THE

Affairs of *FRANCE:*

Purg'd from the Errors and Partiality of *News-Writers* and *Petty-Statesmen,* of all Sides.

Saturday, Feb. 19. 1704.

The INTRODUCTION.

THIS Paper is the Foundation of a very large and useful Design, which, if it meet with suitable Encouragement, *Permissu Superiorum,* may contribute to Setting the Affairs of *Europe* in a Clearer Light, and to prevent the various uncertain Accounts, and the Partial Reflections of our Street-Scriblers, who Daily and Monthly Amuse Mankind with Stories of Great Victories when we are Beaten, Miracles when we Conquer, and a Multitude of Unaccountable and Inconsistent Stories, which have at least this Effect, That People are possest with wrong Notions of Things, and Nations Wheedled to believe Nonsense and Contradiction.

A   A2

[17] Defoe's *A Weekly Review.* 1704.

printed in 1780. Its straightforward text pages are set in a type produced for the Biblioteca Real by Gerónimo Gil. The type used for Yriarte's *Obras Sueltas* is a roman that is the essence of style without fashion. It is an excellent example of continuity in the development of roman as first expressed by Jenson and Aldus and carried forward by Tory and Garamond. It is to be noted that the capitals retain the inscriptional quality of sixteenth-century models when so many designs were giving way to the corrupted forms made fashionable with the spread of intaglio.

Defoe, Steele, and Addison

Early in the eighteenth century, three new periodicals in England introduced a significant dimension into journalism. In the shaping of *The Review* (1704), *The Tatler* (1709), and

[18] *The Spectator.* 1711.

The Spectator (1711), three archetypal English journalists emerged—Daniel Defoe, Richard Steele, and Joseph Addison. Not only do they live today wherever English literature is taught, but they are present in spirit in many newspaper columns and magazine articles.

Defoe's *The Review* was originally called *A Weekly Review of the Affairs of France*. It was issued three times weekly and continued until 1713, with most of the material written by Defoe. Although *The Review* was called nonpartisan, opinion was expressed on many current topics—a forerunner of the editorial. As early as 1703, Defoe was fined and imprisoned for *The Shortest Way with Dissenters*, a pamphlet attacking ecclesiastical intolerance. After a number of brushes with authority, he became cynical to the point where he hired his pen out to causes in which he had no emotional involvement. His genius, however, outweighed his cynicism. In 1719, he produced *Rob-*

A Short History of the Printed Word

inson Crusoe. It was the first story to be published serially.

Steele's *Tatler* appeared three times a week, until 1711. It purported to be written from various coffeehouses. An early collaborator in it was Joseph Addison and, in 1711, Steele and Addison joined to found *The Spectator*, as successor to *The Tatler*. The new publication used the device of a small club to provide types to play the roles of authorship. Among those fictional authors employed by Steele was Bickerstaff. He was borrowed from Isaac Bickerstaff, a 1708 creation of Jonathan Swift. Swift was a friend of Addison and Steele and it may be presumed that he had more influence on *Tatler* and *Spectator* than merely supplying the character of Bickerstaff. The two publications were dedicated to entertainment and enlightenment, and their appeal was great.

[19] *The New England Courant.* 1721.

Newspapers: *America and England*

America's first continuing paper was John Campbell's *Boston News-Letter* of 1704. Campbell was a bookseller who became postmaster at Boston and was able to use his position to gather news from the ships' captains and post riders. This news was then transcribed by his brother, as manuscript newsletters. His issue of April 24, 1704, substituted the printing press for the pen. Campbell's venture was not highly popular; even after years of publication he could report a circulation of only 250 copies. The *News-Letter* was continued by Campbell until 1723, at which time it was acquired by Bartholomew Green, its printer. With two subsequent changes in editorship the paper lasted for more than 70 years, finally disappearing in the Revolution.

In 1719, John Campbell's successor as postmaster established the *Boston Gazette*. His name was William Brooker and he served less than a year in office. He considered the paper to be part of the postmastering job, and this held true for five subsequent postmasters who edited the *Gazette*. It finally became the property of Benjamin Edes and John Gill, Boston printers, who were responsible for directing it toward its eventual role as a leading patriot organ. The first printer of the *Gazette* had been James Franklin, whose apprentice was his younger brother, Benjamin. When Brooker lost the postmastership, the Franklins lost the job of printing the paper. In 1721, James Franklin took on the publication of a newly conceived *New-England Courant*. Despite a short life—only five and a half years—the *Courant*, with its human interest essays, represented a more creative approach to journalism. It did not rely on news alone, which had to be days, weeks, and even months old. Unlike *Publick Occurrences* and the *Gazette*, the *Courant* carried no line: *Published by Authority*. In style, it owed a great deal to the example of Steele and Addison.

In addition to serving from 1718 to 1723 as apprentice to his brother James, Benjamin Franklin contributed his "Do-Good Papers" to the *Courant* in 1722, when he was sixteen years old. The following year, he ran away from Boston and settled in Philadelphia. After a short period in London, where he worked in a printshop, Franklin returned to Philadelphia and started the *Pennsylvania Gazette*, which continued from 1729 until 1766. In 1741, he published the short-lived *General Magazine*. It was to have been the first magazine in the colonies, but became the second when the editor-to-be joined a rival printer to issue *The American Magazine*.

Among early American printers having a part in the first colonial newspapers was William Bradford, who established the first press in Philadelphia in 1693. He later became the official royal printer in New York, and in 1725 began publication of the first newspaper in that colony. It was called *The*

[20] *The Connecticut Courant.* 1764.

New-York Gazette. Bradford's grandson, also named William, published the *Pennsylvania Journal and Weekly Advertiser.* His was a strong voice in opposition to the Stamp Act, and he was to be the printer to the first Continental Congress.

Between 1725 and 1764, newspapers were begun in Charleston, South Carolina (1731), Williamsburg, Virginia (1736), New Bern, North Carolina (1751), Savannah, Georgia (1763), and Hartford, Connecticut (1760)—to locate and date some of the more important ones. In Hartford, *The Connecticut Courant* was brought out by Thomas Green of the famous New England printing family. It became the present Hartford *Courant.* A major event in the history of American journalism occurred in 1735 when John Peter Zenger was

[21] The *Daily Courant.* 1702.

brought to trial for "seditious libels." His acquittal was hailed in England as well as in the colonies as a triumph for liberty and the freedom of the press.

Elizabeth Mallet began publication of the *Daily Courant*, England's first daily newspaper, on March 11, 1702. She encountered financial difficulties, which led to a partnership with Samuel Buckley, a fellow printer. Buckley is given credit for being one of the earliest proponents of high standards of journalistic integrity. He kept the *Courant* successful and in print for thirty years.

Two English papers published before the American Revolution, the *Morning Chronicle* (1769) and the *Morning Post* (1772), provide examples of the quality of contributing writers of the time. The *Chronicle* employed Samuel Taylor Coleridge, William Hazlitt, and Charles Lamb. Robert Southey and William Wordsworth wrote for the *Post*. A third paper, of the same general period, is representative of the crusading press. It was the *North Briton*, founded in 1762 by John Wilkes, who led the fight to allow reporting of news about the government. He achieved some success, but lost his paper and his seat in Parliament in the process. He became something of a hero to the colonial patriots, and the South Carolina Assembly set aside £1,500 to help him pay off the debts resulting from his zeal.

An All-Iron Press

For three and a quarter centuries, the press as designed by Gutenberg had remained virtually unchanged. In 1772, Wilhelm Haas of Basel built one in which all of the parts subject to heavy stress were made of iron, including of course both the platen and the bed. In 1800, Charles, Earl of Stanhope, designed an all-iron press that was used at the Boydell and Nicol Shakespeare Printing Office in London. William Bulmer (1757–1830) was printer for this press, and associated with Bulmer as type-cutter was William Martin, who had worked in the Baskerville foundry.

The chase I sing, hounds, and their various breed,
And no less various use.   O thou, great Prince!
Whom Cambria's towering hills proclaim their lord,
Deign thou to hear my bold, instructive song.
While grateful citizens, with pompous show,
Rear the triumphal arch, rich with the exploits
Of thy illustrious house; while virgins pave
Thy way with flowers, and as the royal youth
Passing they view, admire, and sigh in vain;
While crowded theatres, too fondly proud
Of their exotick minstrels, and shrill pipes,
The price of manhood, hail thee with a song,

·[22] Illustration by Bewick for *The Chase*. 1796.

William Bulmer and Thomas Bewick

Bulmer was born in Newcastle, where from an early age he had known Thomas Bewick, who is regarded as the father of wood engraving. Bewick made blocks for several books before he began his association with Bulmer, but it was Bulmer who provided the knowledge and craftsmanship to show the new technique of block-making to its best advantage.

Bewick was apprenticed, at the age of fourteen, to Ralph

Beilby, a copperplate engraver. His early work was not in the field of printing, but in the rougher work of engraving door-plates and sword blades. During his apprenticeship he had some opportunities to work on wood, and his results were generally praised, partly because of the low ebb to which most work in the medium had sunk. By 1790 his *General History of Quad-rupeds* had established him and his method. Later, in 1795 and 1796, with his engravings for *Poems* by Goldsmith and Parnell, and *The Chase* by Somerville—both printed by Bulmer—Bewick was given the typography and the presswork he needed.

Wood Engraving

Wood engraving as practiced by Bewick represented a new technique, and it played an important role in every kind of illustration printed in letterpress from the end of the eighteenth century until the successful introduction of photoengraving nearly a century later. Instead of the plank, wood engraving required a cross section of the tree. Boxwood was the preferred material. As late as 1766, Papillon, the famous French wood-cutter and author of a manual of techniques, belittled stories he had heard of using a graver upon the end grain of box.

The new practice of wood engraving became known as "white line." The phrase described a method of producing shapes and tints that was not unlike drawing on a blackboard with chalk rather than substituting graver for knife and working toward a facsimile of a drawing. Turkish boxwood has been the most satisfactory source of end-grain wood, and to obtain a

[23] Graver for working on endgrain wood.

block of any great size requires gluing sections together. There was always the danger that the sections would open up.

Gravers for wood engraving are much like those used for metal. The curved shape of the tools facilitates the lifting of the point. Since wood, being less hard than metal, has less tendency to cause a graver to hang, the tool used on wood can have a more acute point than one meant for copper or steel. In both instances, the work is turned and the tool is so held that the thrust of a stroke is delivered from the pad of the palm, with the thumb as guide and rest, rather than from the fingers.

[24] The manner of holding a graver.

Putting the design on the block is no different from preparing a woodcut. One of the hazards in working with gravers is the danger of *leaning*—pressing on a delicate line with the belly of the tool. Sometimes the wood can be made to swell and restore itself by applying a touch of saliva. To make a repair or a correction, a hole is drilled in the block and a plug of wood inserted and resurfaced.

Bewick did his own engraving and therefore had complete freedom to choose the way in which he created his various textures and tones. He was also able to make use of some of the tricks of block-printing, where sections are "lowered" to cause them to print with a grayer effect, or, through the use of overlays, pressures at given points can be stressed and thus provide accents in the print. Such operations require both understanding and cooperation from the pressman.

Revolutions: Political and Industrial

The last half of the century was a period of political, social, and economic revolution. The American Revolution ended colonial status and dependence on England. Efforts to make type in America had been of little consequence. Benjamin Franklin's attempts to set his grandson up as a founder were not successful. Such equipment as he had was finally a part of the Philadelphia operation of Archibald Binney and James Ronaldson, two Scots who began there in 1796. Their first type showing was also the first by an American foundry; it was not issued until 1809. The stock and condition of type faces in America were such that Franklin complained of being nearly blinded from trying to read the Boston newspapers that had been sent to him.

In France, the revolution was violent, yet the storming of the Bastille, in 1789, came only six years after Didot's printing of *Les Aventures de Télémaque*. The work of both Fournier and Didot represented an industry in a high state of orderly development since France had maintained typographic leadership for most of two centuries.

The Industrial Revolution began in England around the middle of the eighteenth century and continued for one hundred years. James Watt's invention of the steam engine in 1769 led to a series of major changes in the textile industry, with a power loom appearing in 1783. Thus far, printing had continued to be a handcraft. Presses were still manually operated and in principle were little altered since the time of the incunabula. Type was still set by hand and had to be printed from and redistributed on the basis of the supply in a printer's cases. No printer had a sufficient number of characters to take care of the composition of a text of any length. Thus the pressures for better solutions were steadily increasing.

Artists: Literary and Graphic

The literary artists who were creating the raw material for

Sommeille en paix ma chere Annette;
Hélas! c'eſt pour moi seul que sont faits tous les maux.

[25] Moreau engraving for *Chansons*.

eighteenth-century printers exhibited a strong affinity for journalism and pamphleteering. Jonathan Swift, Jean Jacques Rousseau, Tom Paine, and Voltaire are among the great and familiar names. Periodicals and newspapers claimed, besides Daniel Defoe, Joseph Addison, and Richard Steele, such contributors as Charles Lamb, William Hazlitt, William Wordsworth, Robert Southey, and Samuel Taylor Coleridge. This was also the century of Oliver Goldsmith, Alexander Pope, and Samuel Johnson. In Germany, by 1795, Goethe had published *Faust* and *Wilhelm Meisters Lehrjahre*, the latter printed by

A Short History of the Printed Word

[26] Hogarth engraving for *Tristram Shandy*.

Johann Friedrich Unger, whose name is connected with simpli-
fying the form of *Fraktur*. ✳ see p.63

One of the most prolific illustrators of the century was a
German, Daniel Nikolaus Chodowiecki, an artist-engraver
who was born in 1726 and died in 1801. He made illustrations
for works by Shakespeare, Cervantes, Goethe, Sterne, Voltaire,
and numerous other authors. After him, the French group that
did portraiture, decorations, theatricals, and special publications
for the court represents the typical rococo illustrations of the

CHAPTER VII · *The Eighteenth Century*   169 century: Boucher, Moreau le jeune, Cochin, Eisen, and Gravelot. An example of Moreau's style is his illustration for Laborde's *Chansons*, published in 1773.

Three of the great artists of the century, all with outstanding capacities as illustrators, were not generally employed for books. Nevertheless, each of them influenced illustration more than those artists who were more regularly commissioned. William Hogarth did only two books, *Hudibras* and *Tristram Shandy*. Fragonard's remarkable set of studies for *Orlando Furioso* never got as far as the engravers. The third graphic master was Francisco Goya. The *Caprichos* that he announced in 1797 represent one of the great graphic achievements of the century of intaglio, and closed it with as vivid a set of narrative prints as the medium has ever produced.

CHAPTER VIII

The Nineteenth Century

I N THE CLOSING YEARS of the eighteenth century, when Bewick was perfecting his white-line style of engraving on end-grain wood blocks, a young Bavarian writer stumbled on a printing process that was neither relief nor intaglio. His name was Aloys Senefelder. He was born in 1771, the son of a Munich actor. Senefelder tried his hand at writing plays, and when he was unable to get them published began a series of efforts to become his own printer. His first trials were engraved and etched on copper, the printing being done on a makeshift intaglio press.

The Discovery of Lithography

The high cost of copper led Senefelder to a number of experiments with limestone slate, and in 1796 he succeeded in making an image on stone with an ink mixture that he had prepared as an etching base for his plate work. When he had etched the stone with nitric acid, he produced the image on a slightly raised surface, which he then inked and printed. His problem lay in the difficulty of keeping ink off the spaces around the image. Successive experiments led to Senefelder's discovery that it was not necessary for the printing surface to be raised. The essence of the medium he had come upon was its chemical rather than mechanical basis, depending on affinity and rejection. A greasy image surrounded by a water-attracting surface accepts greasy ink that the dampened parts reject. Senefelder also discovered the special properties of the Solnhofen stones from Bavaria, and by 1798 had designed a workable press for printing from his stones. By 1803 he had succeeded in adapting his process to metal plates, by means of suitable graining. All the essential elements of what after 1804 came to be called lithography were known to its inventor in the first decade after its discovery.

Gutenberg printed from a relief surface. The engravings and etchings that illustrated so many books of the seventeenth and eighteenth centuries were printed from a lowered surface. Lithography prints from a plane or level surface and is therefore referred to as planographic printing. The pressure of a relief printing press is direct contact, that of an intaglio press is a rolling and squeezing pressure, the ink having to be drawn out of the lines. In lithography, the press exerts a scraping pressure, with the image areas greasy and the balance of the areas moist. Each method utilizes successively stiffer inks and greater printing pressures.

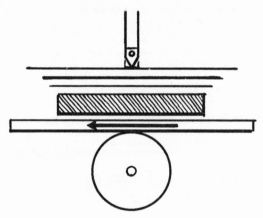

[1] Pressure system for planographic printing.

The principal materials of lithography, besides the stone or zinc, are crayons that range from hard to soft and are made in pencil and stick form. For line work and washes a soluble form of greasy ink, *touche*, is necessary, and can be used with pen, brush and flannel. In addition, there must be some kind of scraper, usually in pencil-like shape. A lithographic stone may be reused many times, the old drawing being removed by a grinding process.

CHAPTER VIII · *The Nineteenth Century*

In 1818, Senefelder wrote and published a manual, *Vollständiges Lehrbuch der Steindruckerei* (Complete Manual of Stone Printing), that has remained the basic text on the subject. Early in his work he had the cooperation of gifted artists in experimenting with possibilities of the medium. One of his earliest patrons was Philipp André, the German music publisher of Offenbach, who took the inventor to England in 1801, where a patent was issued. A book showing specimens of the process appeared in 1803.

The First Power Presses

It has been observed repeatedly that printing presses changed little from the first one used by Gutenberg in the middle of the fifteenth century to those employed in the middle of the eighteenth century. After that, several models were developed with improved delivery of the printing impression and stronger elements throughout, until finally there was the all-iron press designed by Lord Stanhope that was set up at the printing office of William Bulmer. The Industrial Revolution, with new concepts of tools based on new sources of power, could logically be expected to penetrate the area of printing that is most routine and physically demanding. Hand presses are platen presses—a heavy plate is brought against the type form or block. Early attempts to add power to a letterpress machine on the platen principle were not successful, and it was not until the middle of the nineteenth century the problem was solved.

One of the earliest attempts at solving the application of power was made by a German named Friedrich Koenig, and his was called a "Suhler" press because he worked in the Thuringian town of Suhl. When his Suhler press was not successful, Koenig began work on a different principle, a stop-cylinder press. In this, the form was on a flat bed that moved back and forth beneath a cylinder. In the printing sequence the cylinder rotated a third of a revolution, but on the return the cylinder remained stationary, thus affording opportunity for the press-

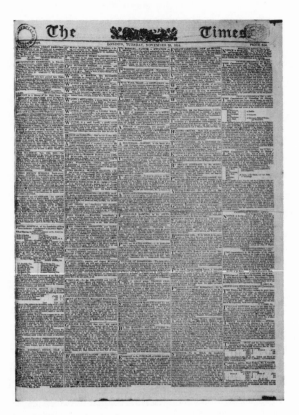

[2] *The* (London) *Times*, the first newspaper printed on a power press. 1814.

man to feed in a fresh sheet of paper. Koenig's first press had a capacity of 800 sheets an hour. Two years later he completed a double press, with two cylinders, each of which handled the impression in one direction of the bed. The inking mechanism was improved and the output was increased to 1,100 sheets an hour. It was this second version that was first used for printing *The Times* of London on November 29, 1814. A third model used cast cylinders for the inking rollers, in place of the earlier leather ones. Grippers were introduced to replace the tapes that had been used to guide the paper.

The first use of a power press, in 1814 by *The Times* of London, marked the beginning of modern printing, best characterized by an emphasis on production. That it took place in a newspaper plant rather than in a large book manufactory is an indication of the contribution made over the past century

A Short History of the Printed Word

and a half to the development of printing by its more ephemeral branches.

However, it is not enough to point to the role of newspapers and magazines in subsidizing the invention and perfecting of large presses, type-composing machines, and methods of reproduction. They deserve also to be credited with providing the chief training ground for writers. In the fifteenth century, printing served scholarship and the Church. As the tool of literacy, the press created its own clientele—so dramatically shown in the rapid spread of printing during the sixteenth and seventeenth centuries. The popular press, as expressed in journalism, provided ready-made circulation for commercial announcements and private notices. In time, advertising helped to shape the economy and appearance of modern newspapers.

There has always been a tendency to equate printing with *fine* printing, for purposes of exploring the past in typography and presswork. To do this is to ignore many of the important forces that helped to shape the use of type. Advertisers, for nearly half a century, have provided the chief support of the foundries that designed and cast display type faces for hand composition, as well as the houses that stocked them and the compositors who set them.

The Foudrinier Paper-Making Machine

Between 1798 and 1806 a machine on which it was possible to make a continuous roll of paper was developed by Nicolas Louis Robert. He was connected with a paper mill at Essonnes, France, that had been started by Pierre François Didot. An English relative of the Didots, John Gamble, took a model of the machine to England, where it was patented. Henry and Sealy Foudrinier, for whom the machine was later named, became interested in it and subsidized its further development by Bryan Donkin, an Englishman.

The Foudrinier machine consists of a vat for pulp, a mesh belt, a suction box, drying and calendering rollers, and a reel. In principle it is the basis for modern paper-making equipment.

The pulp, in an extremely wet state, flows from the vat, or head box, in an even stream onto the Foudrinier wire belt that travels continuously in a direction away from the wet end. The forward motion is accompanied by a side-to-side vibration that crisscrosses the pulp fibers and strengthens the material. On either side of the wet pulp, moving deckle straps keep the pulp from spilling over. Suction boxes then draw out the extra moisture. The formed substance is next run through felt-covered cylinders, called couch rolls. After this compacting and drying, the pulp is continued on a felt belt to a series of hot cylinders. Finally, in the calender stack the roll of paper is given a smooth finish. Each of the machine's actions is comparable to a phase of the hand operation. The final finishing is, of course, a development of Bulmer's hot-pressing. The resulting paper is *wove*, i.e., without any pattern, either laid marks or watermarks. When marks are required they must be lightly impressed, during the wet state, by a *dandy roll*, a cylinder the width of the machine carrying the pattern of the mark in relief. The larger rolls of paper are finally slit into rolls of the desired widths, which in turn can be cut into sheets.

Stereotyping

During the eighteenth century, and especially toward its end, a means of casting from set type and blocks was evolving. As early as 1727, William Ged, of Edinburgh, invented a means of pressing a type form into material that could then be used as a matrix to make a casting duplicating the form. Ged's invention was strongly opposed by the printers of his time, but in 1794, Firmin Didot became interested in the machine and experimented with the inventions of Ged and others. It was Didot who gave the process its name: *stereotype*, the prefix "stereo" describing the solidity of the printing unit.

In addition to saving the original type from wear, and eliminating the possibility of individual pieces of type becoming loose and working up, stereotypes provided the means of putting an entire book into type before printing, and of reprinting at will. The earliest material used for the matrix was *flong*—alternate layers of blotting paper and tissue. This material has been used both wet and dry. In 1804, Lord Stanhope devised a more sensitive method, using plaster. It was not until 1830, however, that the present *papier-mâché* method was used, in Paris. In 1816, William Nicholson made the first attempts to produce curved stereotypes that could be fitted to cylinders; half a century later his ideas took hold and were put into general use. Stereotype metal, from which the casting duplicating the type form is made by means of the matrix, is an alloy of tin, antimony, and lead.

In 1837, electrotyping, an improved method of duplicating printing forms, was perfected. The original type or block was pressed into a waxy slab, and the resulting mold was dusted with graphite and put in a galvanic bath, and a shell of copper was precipitated into the depressions. Finally, the shell was backed with type metal and blocked to be made type-high.

Neo-Classicism

Lithography, mechanical presses, machine-made paper, and stereotypes all belong to the techniques and materials of printing. The appearance of printing is eventually influenced in some way by technical developments, and not necessarily those that are contemporary. The first of the two chief influences in the eighteenth century was intaglio, as interpreted by Grandjean in his *romain du roi*, Luce, Baskerville, Fournier, Bodoni, and the Didots. This direction continued into the nineteenth century with even more stress on the engraved look of the alphabets. The second influence was the classic revival that found expression in all the arts. It had been stimulated throughout most of the eighteenth century by Roman excavations, notably at Pompeii and Herculaneum, and by the beginning of archeological studies in Greece in 1751. James Stuart, an English architect-painter, and Nicholas Revett made careful measurements of the Acropolis and these were published, along with illustrations, in a book entitled *Antiquities of Athens*.

The Roman phase of Neo-classicism was a dominant force in shaping the style known as Empire. Napoleon's invasion of northern Italy in 1796 reinforced French interest in Roman antiquity. The Dukes of Parma and Modena, the Pope, and the King of Naples purchased truces with money and art treasures. The ever-fortunate Bodoni fared well at the hands of the invaders. He received pensions from both Eugène de Beauharnais, Viceroy of Naples, and Napoleon, and a medal was awarded to him in Paris. He died in 1818, and five years later his widow and his shop foreman, Luigi Orsi, published the final edition of Bodoni's *Manuale Tipografico*. It was an outstanding work of type-specimen printing.

Quousque

Quousque

Quousque

[3] Three weights of Bodoni's *ducale* size, from the *Manuale Tipografico*. 1818.

The Didots

The remarkable Didot family, having begun in typography and publishing in 1713, continued into the nineteenth century with great distinction in printing and every field related to it: founding, stereotyping, and paper-making. The two sons of François Ambroise, Pierre l'âiné and Firmin, were particularly active. Firmin took over the operation of his father's foundry and is credited with the type used in his brother's éditions du Louvre *Racine*. This type design has severe contrasts between thick and thin strokes, and produces an effect of sharpness that does not serve the proper end of legibility. In 1811, Firmin

Didot began cutting a type for the Imprimerie Impériale with body sizes based on the metric system.

Pierre Didot's *Racine* was printed in three folio volumes and contained fifty-seven engraved illustrations by a group of well-known artists. One hundred and fifty copies were printed, at a subscription price of 1,800 francs. Like the publications issued by Bodoni at Parma, the éditions du Louvre of Didot could hardly be taken as a measure of the state of printing in the early nineteenth century. Bodoni made no secret of his interest in the appearance of his publications, rather than in their usefulness. He was criticized for his careless editing and lack of attention to scholarly detail, even by Horace Walpole, an admirer for whom he did some printing.

SPECIMEN

DES

NOUVEAUX CARACTÈRES

DE LA FONDERIE ET DE L'IMPRIMERIE
DE P. DIDOT, L'AINÉ,
CHEVALIER DE L'ORDRE ROYAL DE SAINT-MICHEL,
IMPRIMEUR DU ROI ET DE LA CHAMBRE DES PAIRS,

DÉDIÉ

À JULES DIDOT, FILS,
CHEVALIER DE LA LÉGION D'HONNEUR.

À PARIS,

CHEZ P. DIDOT, L'AINÉ, ET JULES DIDOT, FILS
RUE DU PONT DE LODI, Nº 6.

MDCCCXIX

[4] Title page for specimen issued by the foundry of Pierre Didot l'aîné. 1819.

Quousque tandem abutere, Catilina, patientia nostra? quamdiu nos etiam furor iste tuus eludet?
quem ad finem sese effrenata jactabit audacia?
nihilne te nocturnum præsidium palatii, nihil urbis vigiliæ, nihil timor populi, nihil consensus bonorum omnium, nihil hic munitissimus habendi
senatus locus, nihil horum ora vultusque moverunt?
A B C D E F G H I J K L M N O P Q R S T U V
A B C D E F G H I J K L M N O P Q R S T U V W X Y Z
£ 0 1 2 3 4 5 6 7 8 9

*Quousque tandem abutere, Catilina, patientia nos-
tra? quamdiu nos etiam furor iste tuus eludet?
quem ad finem sese effrenata jactabit audacia? nihilne te nocturnum præsidium palatii, nihil urbis
vigiliæ, nihil timor populi, nihil consensus bonorum
omnium, nihil hic munitissimus habendi senatus
locus, nihil horum ora vultusque moverunt; patere*
A B C D E F G H I J K L M N O P Q R S
A B C D E F G H I J K L M N O P Q R S T U V W X Y Z Æ Œ

[5] Modern face from Alexander Wilson & Sons. 1833.

England: The Modern Style and a Counterrevolution

French type founding was dominated by the Didot style
during the first half of the nineteenth century. The alphabet
cut in 1818 by Jacquemin and later one by Legrand are essentially bold and condensed versions of Firmin Didot's classical
modern of 1811. In England, at the beginning of the century,
there were several printers of note: Bulmer, Bensley, Bell, and
Johnson. Thomas Bensley worked in London and was known
for his careful presswork. An example of it is *The Grave*, by
Robert Blair, published in 1813 by Ackermann with illustrations by William Blake. John Bell, type founder, publisher, and
bookseller, is known today through the revived version of Bell,
the letter cut for him by Richard Austin. Bell represents the
beginning of modern, and it is interesting to note that the
punch-cutter Austin worked later for the Glasgow foundry of
Alexander Wilson and Sons, where Scotch Modern, a face still
in wide use, was produced.

Quousque tandem abutere, Catilina, patientia
nostra? quamdiu nos etiam furor iste tuus eludet? quem ad finem sese effrenata jactabit audacia? nihilne te nocturnum præsidium palatii
ABCDEFGHIJKLMNOPQRSTUVWXYZ
ÆŒ£1234567890
ABCDEFGHIJKLMNOPQRSTUVWXYZÆŒ

Quousque tandem abutere, Catilina, patientia
nostra? quamdiu nos etiam furor iste tuus elu-
det? quem ad finem sese effrenata jactabit au-
dacia? nihilne te nocturnum præsidium palatii

[6] English No. 2. Modern face from William Thorowgood. 1824.

A counterreaction to Neo-classicism and the modern styl-
ized types was led by William Pickering, an English publisher
associated with the younger Charles Whittingham, printer, of
the Chiswick Press. It was Pickering who, in 1823, introduced
the use of cloth for binding books. In 1844, he commissioned
the Caslon foundry to cast fonts of the original Caslon *Old
Face*. At that time, the English foundries were promoting a
number of type faces and ornaments reflecting the worst of the
Bodoni and Didot styles. An example is the fat modern roman
offered by William Thorowgood. Pickering found much of
his inspiration in work of the French printers of the sixteenth
century, but he chose to work with a type that was not so old
as that, and was English via Holland rather than Italy or
France. He borrowed the dolphin and anchor, Aldus's mark,
and added "English disciple of Aldus" in Latin. His first publication in revived Caslon was a fictional journal laid in the seventeenth century and entitled *The Diary of Lady Willoughby*.

Illustration

If the books of the early nineteenth century were often
barren typographically, they add up to a rich harvest of outstanding graphic art in the form of illustrations. From the early
seventeenth century on, there was a steady increase in the

her Cheeke by fome Query refpecting a particular Piece of Needle-work in hand; and
added, on perceiving the Effect fhe had produced, fhe had heard *S*r. *Erafmus de la Foun-
tain* much commend the delicate Paterne:
whereat poore *Margaret* attempted to look up
unconcern'd, but was obliged to fmile at her
Sifter's·Pleafantry. I was difcreet, and led the
Converfation back to the Spinning.

The Days paffe fmoothly, yet Time feemeth
very long fince my deare *Lord* departed on his
Journey. We heare no News. *Armftrong* will
perchance gain fome Tydings at *Colchefter:*
and I muft await his Return with fuch Patience
I can.

Since my little *Fanny's* long Sickneffe I have
continued the Habit of remaining by her at
night, fometime after fhe is in Bed: thefe are
Seafons peculiarly fweet and foothing; there
feemeth fomething holy in the Aire of the
dimly lighted *Chamber*, wherein is no Sound
heard

[7] Pickering's revival of Caslon *Old Face.* 1844.

importance of the role of illustration in book publishing. The
engraver of the seventeenth century succeeded in determining
the nature of type in the eighteenth and nineteenth. Intaglio
engraving continued to be popular and it was made more practical in 1818 by Heath and Perkins, who collaborated in developing etching and engraving on steel. This greatly lengthened
the life of the plate.

As lithography was mastered by more and more artists—
Eugène Delacroix's great lithographs for *Faust* in 1828 and

[8] Delacroix lithograph for *Faust*. 1828.

Honoré Daumier's for the Paris press are notable examples—
that medium began to influence letterpress style, and in lesser
hands, not for the better. It was in the nature of Senefelder's
process for doodling to be easy, and since the craftsmen who
lettered on stone were seldom inspired calligraphers, the results
were often pedestrian.

Although photography was being developed—both Da-
guerre and Talbot were at work as early as 1833—only in the
latter quarter of the century was it a factor in making reproduction plates for printing. Around 1850, a Frenchman named
Firmin Gillot made relief etchings of high enough quality, but
the chief means of reproduction at mid-century continued to
be wood, metal engraving, and lithography. In some instances,
artists were able to translate their own drawings on to wood,
metal, or stone. In time, when offset, a cheaper and faster
outgrowth of lithography, had been perfected, it won a good

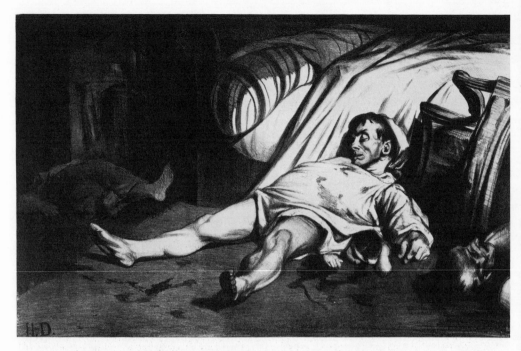

[9] Daumier lithograph. *Rue Transnonain*. 1834.

part of its popularity because of its usefulness in reproducing
pictorial material.

Illustrators: England

A unique figure among the illustrators and bookmakers of
the late eighteenth and early nineteenth centuries was William
Blake, who was born in London in 1757. At an early age he was
given lessons in drawing, and at fourteen was apprenticed to an
engraver with whom he worked for seven years. Blake studied
at the Royal Academy but was unhappy with the atmosphere
he found there and left to set up as an engraver on his own. His
complete individuality and mysticism contributed to his failure
to win a popular following. Twin inspirations, art and poetry,
forced him to find a means of making his own books, and the
solution was to draw the designs and write the words on copper
with an acid-resisting liquid, and etch away the light areas with
nitric acid. The first of his books was the *Songs of Innocence* of
1789, and the last completed work was the illustrations for the

A Short History of the Printed Word

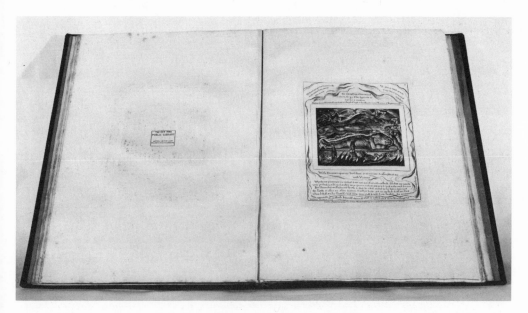

[10] Blake. *The Book of Job.* 1826.

Book of Job of 1826, two years before he died.

Blake's relief-etched books may be considered as updated block books. So little were they understood and valued at the time that he would have died in poverty had not an admirer

[11] Blake. Wood engravings for *Virgil.* 1821.

[12] Rowlandson. Aquatint illustration for *The Vicar of Wakefield*.

commissioned him to do the *Book of Job*. A measure of the contemporary taste is shown in an explanatory note to Blake's wood engravings for Thornton's *Eclogue of Virgil*, published in 1821:

The illustrations of this English Pastoral are by the famous Blake, the illustrator of Young's Night Thoughts *and Blair's* Grave, *who designed and engraved them himself. This is mentioned, as they display less of art than genius, and are much admired by some eminent painters.*

Thomas Rowlandson was another of the graphic artists who bridged the two centuries. He was born in London just a year before Blake, but he was in no sense a visionary like his great contemporary. Instead, he was a combination of caricaturist and social reporter, and, as such, a forerunner of the English school of illustrators associated especially with the development of the magazine *Punch*. Rowlandson's medium was aquatint, for which he did the outline drawings and left the tones to be laid in by specialists. The prints were hand-colored,

A Short History of the Printed Word

[13] Cruikshank. Etched illustration for *Oliver Twist*. 1838.

often by children. Among his characteristic illustrations are those for *The Vicar of Wakefield*.

A third influential English illustrator of the time was George Cruikshank, who was born in 1792. His productive career embraced almost seven decades, from 1809 to 1877. Some of his work was engraved on wood, but a large portion of it, especially the more familiar illustrations, was etched. Between 1824 and 1826, he made designs for *German Popular Stories* by the Grimm Brothers. These, and his etchings on steel for *Oliver Twist* and other works by Dickens, remain the classic ones. *Oliver Twist* appeared first—in parts—in *Bentley's Miscellany*, and appeared in book form in 1838. Serial publication became the usual practice of the great Victorian novelists, and it testifies to the increasing general literacy as well as to a desire on the part of authors to find ways of enlarging their paying audience.

Illustrators: France and Germany

The giant of French illustration was Honoré Daumier, born in Marseilles in 1808 and taken to Paris in 1814. In 1831, he met Charles Philipon, the liberal publisher of *La Caricature* and *Le Charivari*, and they began a lifetime of collaboration. Daumier did a number of vignettes that appeared in books, and, despite the artist's disappointment with some of the engravings of his work, many of the blocks produced in the 1840's remain classics among illustrations made on wood. Baudelaire said of Daumier that "he drew because he had to—it was his ineluctable vocation." Below, a vignette from *Physiologie du Robert Macaire*, 1842, likely engraved by Birouste.

[14] Daumier. Wood-engraved illustration for *Robert Macaire*. 1842.

Gavarni (pseudonym of Guillaume Sulpice Chevalier) lacked the genius of his contemporary, Daumier, but was an illustrator of note as well as an outstanding practitioner of the techniques of lithography. Among the books he contributed to

[15] Menzel. Wood-engraved illustration for *Frederick the Great*.

is *Les François Peints par Eux-Mêmes*, 1848. Gavarni was sufficiently admired in his own time to have been chosen as the subject of an extensive biography by the Goncourt Brothers.

Paul Gustave Doré might be called the French Cruikshank, and they were friends toward the end of the Englishman's life. In the beginning, Doré executed his own blocks, but success led him to seek the collaboration of some of the best wood engravers of his day. Especially familiar are his illustrations for Balzac's *Contes Drolatiques*, Paris, 1855.

Adolph Menzel also had a group of engravers who were as able as any of their period. During the 1840's, Menzel illustrated Kugler's *Geschichte Friedrichs des Groszen* as well as a number of works by the Emperor Friedrich himself. Among those whose names are associated with engraving the Menzel blocks were Friedrich Ludwig Unzelmann and his student, Eduard Kretzschmar, two of the most brilliant craftsmen who ever worked with wood blocks.

New Presses: Letterpress and Lithography

Experiments were going forward in the direction of substituting a rotary motion for presses, instead of the back and forth traversing of Koenig's cylinder press. In 1846, Richard Hoe patented a rotary sheet press in New York. It was made practical by the improvement of stereotyping that could produce curved plates. That and a continuous roll of paper were adapted by William Bullock and successfully demonstrated in 1865. Ten years later a four-cylinder perfecting press (simultaneously printing on both sides of the paper) was built by J. G. A. Eickhoff.

In 1851 a mechanical press for lithography was built in Vienna by George Sigl. It worked on a principle similar to Koenig's stop-cylinder press. There were improvements, in 1875, to allow for printing on tin by means of offsetting. Offset lithography on paper, however, was not achieved until the early years of the twentieth century.

Typesetting: Linotype and Monotype

Two of the basic mechanical printing developments of the last quarter of the nineteenth century were the invention of the *Linotype* machine, by Ottmar Mergenthaler in 1886, and the *Monotype*, by Tolbert Lanston, in 1893. Both of the machines set and cast copy. Linotype was cast on a slug, Monotype was cast as individual letters and assembled in lines. With Linotype, it was cheaper to produce a first proof, but Monotype provided easier means of correction.

Many attempts were made to develop mechanical aids for compositors. Chiefly, these were assorting or assembling de-

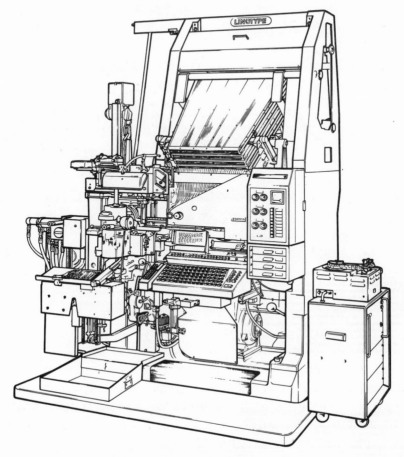

[16] Linotype machine.

vices. As early as 1830, there was progress in improving casting methods for hand composition. By 1862, a type-casting machine was built that could produce completely finished letters ready for the printer's cases.

The Linotype machine requires only a single operator. It has a composing mechanism with a keyboard resembling that of a typewriter. It assembles the matrices from the magazines in which they are stored. The casting mechanism justifies the line —adds the necessary spacing to fill the line—and then casts it. A distributing mechanism returns the matrices to the magazine.

Ottmar Mergenthaler, the inventor of the Linotype, was a

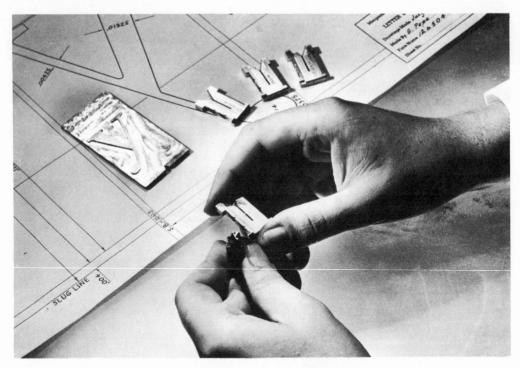

[17] Linotype pattern drawing, pattern, mats, and punch.

German-American who was born in Stuttgart in 1854 and emigrated to the United States when he was eighteen. He lived first in Washington, then went to Baltimore, where he met Charles Moore, the inventor of a typewriting machine for use in making lithographic transfers, and J. O. Clephane, a court reporter, who became his chief financial backer. Mergenthaler's first mechanical typesetting machine was invented in 1884, but the first production model was that used in 1886 by the *New York Tribune*. However, it was not until 1890 that Mergenthaler achieved his goal with the Simplex Linotype.

The importance of such a typesetting device went far beyond its contribution to speeding up composition. The machine *cast* type as well as set it, and the fact that it cast a line at a time made composition easier to handle and kept individual letters from working up. In addition, it provided a printer the equivalent of an inexhaustible type case. With the Linotype, type became disposable, and every job that was reset was made up of fresh type.

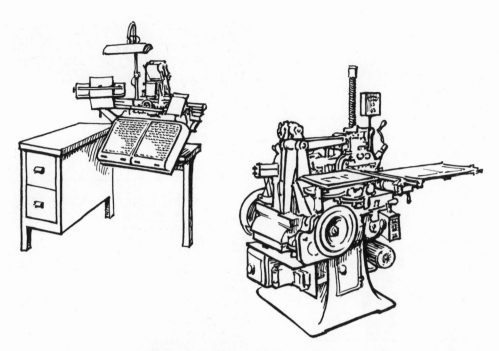

[18] Monotype keyboard and caster.

It was not to be expected that so much could be gained without some significant losses. The price paid was that of flexibility in accepting designs, for, like its cousin the typewriter, the Linotype system imposes various restrictions on the possible shapes of letters. When more than one letter form is on a single mat, the restriction is especially evident.

A Monotype machine consists of two units—a keyboard and a caster—each requiring an operator. The basic principle of operation is the preparation of a perforated tape on the keyboard. This is fed into the caster and there controls a series of compressed air pipes that carry out the selection of matrices. The casting is done letter by letter. The letters are cooled and assembled in a channel until a line is completed.

Tolbert Lanston, the inventor of the Monotype machine, was originally a lawyer. He was born in Troy, Ohio, in 1844. His first machine was exhibited at the Columbian World's Fair in 1893, and in 1899 it was given the improvements that were the basis of the Monotype so popular for good book work during the first three or four decades of the twentieth century.

CHAPTER VIII · *The Nineteenth Century*

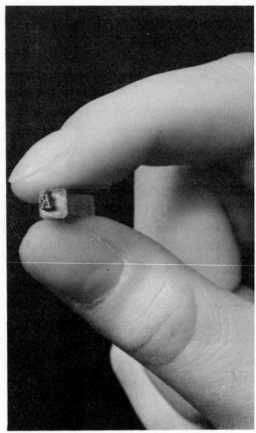

[19] Monotype mats and punch.

The Development of Photoengraving

Firmin Gillot was a pioneer in developing etched metal relief plates for letterpress printing. In the early experiments of Gillot and his predecessors, designs were put on metal by transfer methods similar to lithography. By 1870, the technique of making line blocks or cuts on zinc, using photography, was well advanced, and, by 1880, the process of breaking up tones into dots by photographing the original through wire or glass screens had been invented. Zinc was used for simple linecuts as early as 1840. Copper was preferred for halftones—those works photographed through screens—because of its slower and more controllable etching qualities.

A Short History of the Printed Word

In making a photoengraving, the original is photographed and the negative of this is used to make an acid-resisting positive on metal. The etching of a line block is done in stages, between each of which the image, in relief, is inked to preserve its acid-resisting qualities. At the heart of photomechanical reproduction is photography itself, and the work of Niepce, Talbot, Maddox, Pretsch, and others led to concurrent progress in photogravure, intaglio, and photolithography. In the last category, planographic printing, discoveries by W. H. Fox Talbot were utilized in making a gelatin printing surface that could be used for finely detailed reproductions and that required no screen. The process, called collotype, utilizes glass as the base for the gelatin film.

Nineteenth-Century Newspapers and Magazines

In 1785, John Walter launched *The Daily Universal Register*. Three years later it became *The* (London) *Times*. In spite of Walter's success in providing a better job of reporting than the competition, he continuously faced financial difficulties and began to take bribes from officials and private persons who feared exposure. His son, John Walter II, became publisher of the paper in 1803, and it quickly responded to his moral and economic ministrations. A good part of the credit for the superior foreign news reporting in the *Times* was due to the leadership of Henry Crabb Robinson as foreign news chief. He had served as a foreign correspondent himself, and was a man of distinguished attainments. By 1841, the paper's circulation had reached 30,000 through powerpress printing.

Nineteenth Century: English Magazines

In 1841, *Punch, or the London Charivari* was founded by Ebenezer Landells, a draftsman and wood-engraver. Landells had worked with Bewick, and had in turn taught Edmund Evans, the engraver and printer of the famous color illustrations for children by Randolph Caldecott, Kate Greenaway, and Walter Crane. The inspiration for *Punch* would seem to have been the famous French radical publication *Le Charivari*, edited by Charles Philipon, whose most famous collaborator was Honoré Daumier, generally considered to be the greatest of all political caricaturists.

Landell's proposal for an illustrated magazine, to be named *Punch*, attracted a brilliant list of contributors. Chiefly under the editorial direction of Henry Mayhew, contributors included Thomas Hood and William Makepeace Thackeray, among the authors, and John Leech and John Tenniel, among the artists. Tenniel, who is famous as the illustrator of *Alice in Wonderland*, drew more than 2,000 cartoons for *Punch* during his years as chief political cartoonist. Fifty-odd years later, Ernest Shepard, who served in the same capacity for the magazine, achieved a fame almost as great with his illustrations for A. A. Milne's juveniles about *Winnie the Pooh*.

Bentley's Miscellany, the publication in which Charles Dickens's *Oliver Twist* appeared, with illustrations by George Cruikshank, was begun in 1837 by Richard Bentley, and Dickens was its editor. In 1850, Dickens started a weekly called *Household Words*. Many of his works appeared for the first time in that periodical. Contributors also included Sir Edward Bulwer-Lytton, Charles Lever, Wilkie Collins, and Mrs. Gaskell.

Another of the notable literary periodicals of the mid-nineteenth century was the *Cornhill Magazine*, a monthly founded in 1860 with Thackeray as its editor. Some of Anthony Trollope's novels appeared in the *Cornhill*, along with works by John Ruskin, Matthew Arnold, and, naturally, its editor.

Earlier in the century, in 1802, the *Edinburgh Review* was established by Francis Jeffrey, Henry Brougham, and Sydney Smith. It was a magazine destined to have great influence as a journal of literary criticism. Contributing to the shaping of that influence were Arnold, Thomas Carlyle, Hazlitt, Thomas Babington Macaulay, and Sir Walter Scott. The *Edinburgh Review* survived until 1929.

In 1894, an illustrated quarterly appeared called the *Yellow*

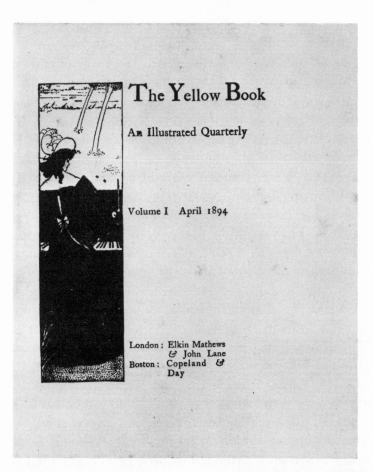

The Yellow Book

An Illustrated Quarterly

Volume I   April 1894

London : Elkin Mathews
        & John Lane
Boston : Copeland &
        Day

[20] *The Yellow Book.* Cover design by Aubrey Beardsley.

Book. It had much in common with little-magazines before and since. Its life was short, only three years. One of its most closely linked contributors was Aubrey Beardsley. The *Yellow Book* printed works by Max Beerbohm, Henry James, and Edmund Gosse, among others.

Nineteenth Century: American Magazines

In the United States, four monthly magazines of deservedly high reputation were launched between 1850 and 1887: *Harper's Monthly Magazine* (1850), *Atlantic Monthly* (1857), *Century Illustrated Monthly Magazine* (1880), and *Scribner's Magazine* (1887).

Harper's was edited for its first six years by Henry Jarvis Raymond (1820–69), who was limited in the time he could devote to the magazine after its first year because he founded *The New York Times* in 1851 with two financiers, George Jones and Edward Wesley. At first, *Harper's* depended largely on British authors: Collins, Dickens, Hardy, Lever, Thackeray, and Trollope. Later, it used works by Mark Twain, Henry James, Herman Melville, and Owen Wister. Among those who illustrated for it were Edwin Abbey, A. B. Frost, Winslow Homer, and Howard Pyle. *Harper's Weekly*, begun in 1857, was the publication for which Thomas Nast, who joined the staff in 1862, created the Tammany tiger, Republican elephant, and Democratic donkey. He also drew the cartoons which helped make the American public aware of the corruption of the Tweed political machine.

The *Atlantic* was named by Oliver Wendell Holmes, who contributed his *Autocrat of the Breakfast-Table* to it. Its first editor was James Russell Lowell. Ralph Waldo Emerson, Henry Wadsworth Longfellow, and James Greenleaf Whittier were among those who wrote for it.

The *Century*, which was an outgrowth of *Scribner's Monthly* (1870–81), provided the first printing of the Lincoln biography by Nicolay and Hay. James's *The Bostonians*, Jack London's *The Sea Wolf*, and Joel Chandler Harris's *Uncle Remus* first appeared in the *Century*. Both *Scribner's Monthly* and the *Century* were well illustrated and well printed.

Scribner's Magazine was started by the younger Charles Scribner after his father had sold *Scribner's Monthly*. It, too, had a remarkable list of authors, among them Robert Louis Stevenson, William and Henry James, Bret Harte, Rudyard Kipling, Stephen Crane, and George Washington Cable. Aside from the quality of their contents, all these magazines had a basic similarity in that they were owned and operated by book publishers.

CHAPTER VIII · *The Nineteenth Century*

The Rise of the American Press

The American press was not handicapped by restrictive special taxation in the nineteenth century and was more free to develop than was the press in England. Bulwer-Lytton pointed out, in the 1830's, that while one in thirty-six bought newspapers in England, one in four bought them in Pennsylvania. However, neither their freedom nor their relatively great numbers and wide circulation kept newspapers in the United States from indulging in a type of crude partisan journalism that delayed their maturing.

An early entry in the nineteenth century was the *New York Evening Post* (1801), which was backed by Alexander Hamilton and was intended to present the Federalist point of view. In 1826, William Cullen Bryant joined the paper and in 1829 became its editor. Bryant moved the *Post* into a position of supporting Jacksonian democracy. Among those associated with the *Post* as editor was Edwin Lawrence Godkin, the great Irish-American liberal who founded *The Nation*.

In 1825, just prior to Bryant's arrival in New York, the *New York Advertiser* became the first American newspaper to use a steam-driven press. It was a Napier, an improved version of the Koenig press used by the London *Times*. Its capacity was 2,000 copies per hour. By 1830, Foudrinier machines were being used in American paper mills, and type foundries had replaced their hand-casting molds with machine casters. Such advances in the mechanics of production help to account for the fact that the five most important New York dailies were begun between 1833 and 1866: the *New York Sun* (1833), the *New York Herald* (1835), the *New York Tribune* (1841), *The New York Times* (1851), and the *New York World* (1866). Only the *Times* has survived.

Benjamin Day started the *Sun* and its most noted editor, after Day, was Charles A. Dana. The *Herald* was founded by James Gordon Bennett and was continued by his son. The younger Bennett also launched the Paris *Herald*. He turned to Richard Harding Davis and Mark Twain for contributions, in addition to conceiving such circulation-building features as Henry M. Stanley's expedition to find David Livingstone. In 1924, the paper was merged with the *Tribune* under the ownership of Ogden Reid. The *Tribune* was founded and edited by Horace Greeley, who was called the greatest journalistic influence in the United States. His tolerance of new ideas helped to make him a constructive crusader. The *World* was begun as a religious newspaper, but attained neither character nor strength until its purchase in 1883 by Joseph Pulitzer.

Raymond, the first editor of *Harper's Monthly*, was also associated with Horace Greeley on the *New York Tribune*. His desire in founding *The New York Times* with Jones and Wesley was to publish a paper that would establish a reputation for accuracy. Raymond continued with the *Times* until his death in 1869. After the death in 1891 of George Jones, who had been the paper's business manager, the standards of the *Times* declined and its circulation went down as well. In 1896, it was purchased by Adolph Ochs and returned to its former position.

The American Point System

In the relatively rapid progress of mechanization that marked printing during the nineteenth century, the United States played a major role, particularly in the invention and development of presses and typesetting machines. The nation's type founders also turned their attention to regularizing typographic measurements. Early in the century George Bruce of New York proposed that the body sizes of types should increase as an arithmetical progression rather than in the haphazard size designations they had come to have in the course of printing history.

The United States Founders Association, in 1886, established a committee to study and formulate a point system for American founders comparable to the Didot system in Europe. The American point system employs a pica unit, which is divided into 12 parts called points. The whole has been related to the metric system on the basis of 83 picas equaling 35 centi-

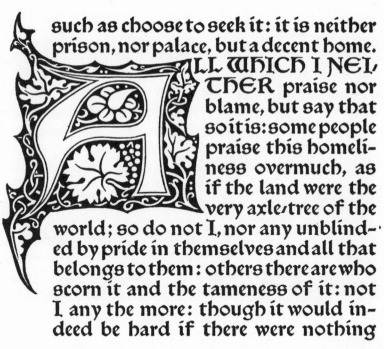

such as choose to seek it: it is neither prison, nor palace, but a decent home. ALL WHICH I NEITHER praise nor blame, but say that so it is: some people praise this homeliness overmuch, as if the land were the very axle-tree of the world; so do not I, nor any unblinded by pride in themselves and all that belongs to them: others there are who scorn it and the tameness of it: not I any the more: though it would indeed be hard if there were nothing

[21] Morris. *Troy* type.

meters. As in the Didot system, the types are identified by their point size.

Caught up in the general zeal for standardization, in 1884 Linn Boyd Benton, inventor of the pantographic punch-cutting machine, led the way in what he called "self-spacing" type, later to be known as "point-set." His purpose was to assure even lines, and to achieve this it was necessary to distort the individual letter forms. An additional regularizing was the introduction of the Standard Lining System, intended to enable type faces of different families and sizes to be aligned more easily. The shop convenience and economic advantage of these "improvements" were bought at high cost to individual letter forms and the effect of the type on the page.

William Morris

Among those who disliked the steady conquest of craftsmanship by the machines was the Englishman William Morris. He was born in 1834 and educated at Oxford, first for the

[22] Morris. The Kelmscott *Chaucer*.

church then for a career in architecture. Finally he took up painting, but was not happy at it and turned to design—as applied to illumination, stained glass, wallpaper, rugs, and furniture. Morris was also interested in writing and produced works of poetry as well as prose throughout his life. Before he started his own shop, his first book had been printed for him by the Chiswick Press, so long associated with the Pickering editions. Morris's socialism and romantic ideas of the nobility of labor were practiced at a safe distance from any knowledge of financial hardship. He had sufficient means to allow him to satisfy his reasonable desires.

Morris set up the Kelmscott Press in 1891. It was named for Kelmscott Manor House, about 30 miles from Oxford, which he had acquired twenty years before. Working with him was Emery Walker, an English engraver and printer who was one of the most versatile designers in English typographic history. Also connected with the Kelmscott editions was the famous punch-cutter Edward Prince, who was generally involved with the types of private presses of the period. Prince cut Morris's *Golden, Chaucer*, and *Troy* types. The printing was done on a hand press, the Albion, devised by Cope in 1823. This press had

A Short History of the Printed Word

a toggle action, to lower the platen, rather than a screw—the final lever principle employed for hand presses.

Morris preached a doctrine of interdependent factors in bookmaking: type, paper, ink, imposition, and impression must be considered together. He regarded two facing pages as the unit. His *Chaucer*, illustrated by his Oxford friend, Edward Burne-Jones, is one of his most highly prized books. It is indeed richly produced. However, in imitating the past, Morris was perhaps doomed to fail in capturing it. This takes nothing from his contribution. Along with his contemporaries, T. J. Cobden-Sanderson with the Doves Press and Charles Ricketts with the Vale Press, Morris called attention to the inherent qualities of all typography and to the basic nature of letterpress printing in particular. He demonstrated that a typographer does not need endless sizes of type, but he needs consistency. It is not the amount of ornament that enhances and gives variety to a page of type, it is the harmony between the two. Above all, he taught those who were interested to learn the value of re-examining the past and to profit by it. When Morris died, in 1896, just five years after setting up the Kelmscott Press, he could hardly have imagined that the influence of his ideas would be so great.

CHAPTER IX

The Twentieth Century: 1900–1940

WHILE THE KELMSCOTT PRESS was still in operation, several other private presses of note were founded in England, among them C. H. St. John Hornby's Ashendene Press and Lucien Pissarro's Eragny Press, both in 1894. In 1900, the Doves Press was set up by T. J. Cobden-Sanderson and William Morris's former associate, Emery Walker. Walker, born in 1851, was one of the most active participants in the typographic revival that began in the 1890's, and before he died, in 1931, he was knighted for his numerous contributions to printing. All of these presses had special types designed for them, and in each case the punch-cutting was executed by Edward Prince of London, who was responsible for the Kelmscott faces.

The United States: Updike, Rogers, and Goudy

Prince also cut three types for Herbert Horne, a designer associated with Morris. Of the three, *Montallegro* had its initial use in Condivi's *Life of Michelagnolo Buonarotti*, printed by the Merrymount Press in Boston. Merrymount was established in 1893 by Daniel Berkeley Updike, one of America's most distinguished and able printers. His two great achievements were the operation of his press as a commercial establishment with impeccable standards and the authorship of his scholarly *Printing Types—Their History, Forms and Use*. Updike was born in 1860 and died in 1941. An example of his work is the opening page of *The Wedding Journey of Charles and Martha Amory*, published in 1922.

Sharing American typographic honors with Updike was

ODI profanum vulgus & arceo;
  Favete linguis: carmina non prius
Audita Musarum sacerdos
  Virginibus puerisq; canto.
Regum timendorum in proprios grege
Reges in ipsos imperium est Iovis,
  Clari Giganteo triumpho,
  Cuncta supercilio moventis.
Est ut viro vir latius ordinet
Arbusta sulcis, hic generosior
  Descendat in Campum petitor,

[1] Hornby. Ashendene Press type.

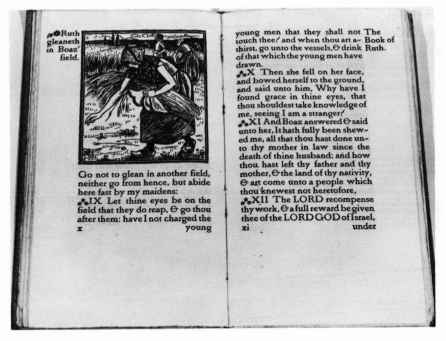

[2] Pissarro. Eragny Press *Book of Ruth and Esther.* 1896.

Bruce Rogers. In 1896, Rogers became designer for the River-side Press in Cambridge, Massachusetts, a subsidiary of the publishing firm of Houghton, Mifflin & Company. He was to become the prototype of the modern free-lance typographer,

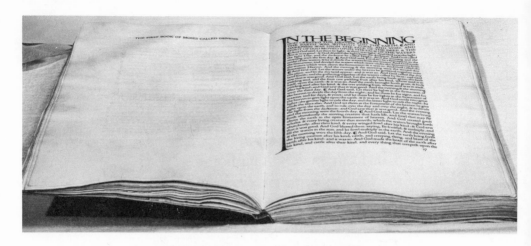

[3] Cobden-Sanderson. Doves Press Bible. 1905.

❡ These Books printed, as a first essay, the whole field of literature remains open to select from. To-day there is an immense reproduction in an admirable cheap form, of all Books which in any language have stood the test of time. But such reproduction is not a substitute for the more monumental production of the same works, & whether by The Doves Press or some other press or presses, such monumental production, expressive of man's admiration, is a legitimate ambition and a public duty. Great thoughts deserve & demand a great setting, whether in building, sculpture, ceremonial, or otherwise; & the great works of literature have again and again to be set forth in forms suitable to their magnitude. And this

[4] Cobden-Sanderson. Doves type.

and in his three-score years of book designing he worked for many publishers, including the Cambridge and Oxford University Presses in England. In 1935, he designed his famous Lectern Bible for Oxford. Rogers was associated for a number of years with the admirable Printing House of William Rudge, at Mt. Vernon, New York, and during his years abroad he worked with Emery Walker. Rogers designed two type faces,

A Short History of the Printed Word

And if you set him beneath as good a man as him
self at the table: that is against his honour. If you
doe not visite him at home at his house: then you
knowe not your dutie. The is maner of fashions and
behaviours, bring men to such scorne and disdaine
of their doings: that there is no man, almost, can
abide to beholde them: for they love them selves

[5] Horne. *Montallegro* type.

Mrs. Amory's Letters

I

Havre, Novr 1st, 1833.

AS I have promised you, my dearest
Mother, an exact account of my "*European experiences,*" I take the first opportunity to commence, after liberation
from sea. You, I am sure, will remem-
ber the 27th of September, when we left
Brookline with you; and our final adieu
at Dedham; that parting scene I shall long remember—such
moments are not easily obliterated from the memory! We
reached Providence to sleep, after a melancholy ride, which,
however, was much enlivened to Mr Amory by Mr E. Preble's
company, who very kindly attended us to N. York, and re-
mained there with us till the eve^g before we sailed. Before
leaving Providence we paid a long visit to our friends the
Arnolds, who received us with even more than their usual
kindnefs. At noon we took pafsage in the Steamboat, where
among others of our acquaintance, we recognized M^r & M^{rs}
N. Amory, who, however, stopped at Newport. In spite of my

[6] Updike. *The Wedding Journey of Charles and Martha
Amory.* 1922.

Montaigne (1901) and *Centaur* (1915), both inspired by Jenson.

In 1903, Frederic W. Goudy, a Midwestern accountant
turned letterer and type designer, set up the Village Press at

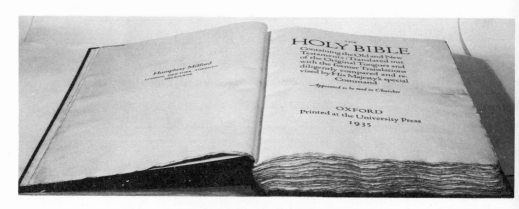

[7] Rogers. Oxford Bible. 1935.

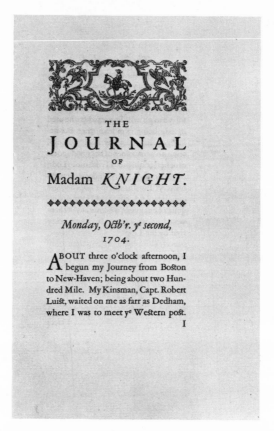

THE

JOURNAL

OF

Madam *KNIGHT*.

*Monday, Octb'r. y*ᵉ* second,*
1704.

ABOUT three o'clock afternoon, I
begun my Journey from Boſton
to New-Haven; being about two Hundred Mile. My Kinsman, Capt. Robert
Luiſt, waited on me as farr as Dedham,
where I was to meet yᵉ Weſtern poſt.

I

[8] Rogers *Journal of Madam Knight.* 1920.

Park Ridge, Ill. Goudy, probably the most prolific type designer in printing history, also produced two books on letters:
The Alphabet and *Elements of Lettering*. He succeeded in

A Short History of the Printed Word

Was born in a cavern of these mountains. Like the river in yonder valley, whose first drops flow from some cliff that weeps in a deep grotto, the first moments of my life sped amidst the shadows of a secluded re- treat, nor vexed its silence. As our mothers draw near their term, they retire to the cav- erns, and in the innermost recesses of the wildest of them all, where the darkness is most dense, they bring forth, uncomplaining, offspring as silent as themselves. Their strength-giving milk enables us to endure with- out weakness or dubious struggles the first difficulties of life; yet

[9] Rogers. *Centaur* type.

The Alphabet

Chapter I. *What Letters Are*

LETTER is a symbol, with a definite shape & significance, indicating a single sound or combination of sounds, and providing a means, through grouping, for the *visible ex- pression* of words—that is, of thoughts.
Originally, letters were adaptations of natural forms employed in picture-writing, but by a process of evolution, [actually degradation,] they have become arbitrary signs with little resemblance to the symbols from which they are derived. These arbitrary shapes have passed through their periods of uncertainty and change; they have a long history and manifold associations; they are classics, and should not be tampered with, except within limits that just discretion may allow.

An ornamental form once found is repeated, the eye grows accustomed to it and expects its recurrence; it becomes established by use; it may be associated with fundamental ideas of life and nature and is handed on and on, until finally its origin and meaning are, perhaps, lost. Just so, the picto- rial significance of individual letters is so deeply buried in oblivion that special study and research would be necessary to resurrect their original form or meaning—an undertaking not essential here.

Language itself, as an organized system, was of necessity slow in devel- oping; the next steps, the approaches toward a more or less phonetic al- phabet, were equally lingering; for speech existed long before it was dis- covered that the human voice could be represented by symbols—thus

[9]

[10] Goudy. Opening page of *The Alphabet*, showing *Ken- nerley* type with a hand-lettered title.

capturing the imagination of American printers as few others have, and his name became familiar in print shops across the country. He came into the field at a time when pantographic engraving machines were beginning to replace hand punch-cutting, and in his later years Goudy turned to such a machine in an attempt to produce his own mats. His results, more often than not, showed traces of overstatement in design, and this tended to reduce their effectiveness for setting any large amounts of text. Among his well-known types is *Kennerley*, named for the publisher of his books on letter design.

Edward Johnston

It seems to me that the one in all that Morris ambience who contributed most to the twentieth-century renaissance in letters was Edward Johnston, an English calligrapher who managed to combine a productive life in ornamental lettering with a remarkable career in teaching, and with the authorship of *Writing and Illuminating, and Lettering*, the outstanding book in the field. It is not likely to be unknown to anyone who has seriously attempted to design letters during the last sixty years. Published in 1906, it has been reprinted more than thirty times. Johnston's pupils included Eric Gill, William Graily Hewitt, and Anna Simons. Close to him in his last years was Alfred Fairbank, a calligrapher and teacher of note. I have asked him to provide a glimpse of his friend:

I recall Edward Johnston as a serious and courteous man, weary from ill health, but with a startling and delightful clarity of mind. He was a perfectionist. Once, too briefly and inadequately, I said to him that I did not believe in perfection. His immediate response was: "I believe in the Book of Kells!" Always he was in search of the Truth and his integrity often caused him to confess defects in his work. His last message to the Society of Scribes and Illuminators was this: "Study your dictionaries. For instance, look up the word 'Authentes' (Greek), one who does things himself, first hand, opposite to

*copied, real, actual, genuine, opposite to pretend, really pro-
ceeding from its reputed source or author."*

*As a calligrapher he was unequalled and his designs of
scripts and inscriptions were an expression of his genius. His
work was mainly based on his belief that the pen with a broad
nib is essentially the letter-making tool. In 1916 he designed the
sans serif of London's Underground railway and thus led attention away from the current Victorian debased designers. His
other type designs, made for Count Kessler, although based
upon the lettera rotunda script of the 15th century and the
italic type used in G. A. Tagliente's writing manual, were*

[11] Kessler. Cranach Press *Virgil*. Title with Maillol
woodcut.

given new life by Johnston's calligraphic knowledge and skill and the cutting of the punches by Edward Prince and, when Prince died, by George Friend.

The English arts and crafts movement, especially as represented by Morris and Johnston, was received with great enthusiasm in Germany. The Count Kessler referred to by Fairbank was Harry Kessler, who was responsible for the Cranach Press

[12] Maillol. *Hamadryads*. Woodcut illustration for *Virgil*.

of Weimar, set up to print *Die Eclogen Vergils*, illustrated by Aristide Maillol. It was to be produced under the direction of Walker, with initials and title lettering by Johnston and Gill. The work, begun in 1912, was interrupted by the war, resumed in 1925, and concluded the following year. Count Kessler planned the volume.

Emery Walker, Edward Johnston, and Eric Gill also contributed the format design and calligraphic title pages to a series of classics printed for the Insel Verlag by Carl Ernst Poeschel early in the century. Poeshel was one of the most distinguished and influential printers in German typographic history, and can be likened to America's Updike. In 1907 he joined Walter Tiemann, an illustrator and typographer, to form the Janus-Presse. They continued to produce books by hand with that imprint until 1923. Tiemann, who illustrated for the Insel Verlag and designed a number of type faces for the Klingspor type foundry in Offenbach, was also the able director of the Leipzig Academy.

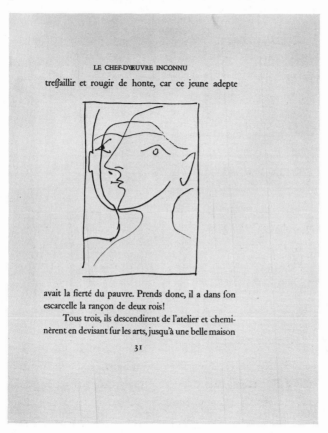

[13] Picasso. Illustration. *Le Chef-d'Oeuvre Inconnu.*

France: Livres de Peintres

In France, the printing revival was directed toward the development of illustrated books, and Ambroise Vollard can be singled out as the publisher contributing most importantly to

Entends donc, Tristes Os, mon pote,
Et vois enfin ce qu'ils ont fait
De cette voix humaine, si belle,

films trop sonores peut-être bien, tant de bruits incongrus que le Préfet d'Athènes a prohibés hier sur beau papier blanc — cela nous a coûté quelques deniers, et ces bruits renaissent plus discordants encore. Le Préfet affirme que tout homme de progrès devra s'y habituer; d'autres assurent mettre au point des disques parfaits, admettons-le, à condition que ce soit ma colombe qui roucoule sur mon cœur en mineur et non les aboyeurs de la Bourse de Paris par haut-hurleur. La vie est amère et ce peuple, dont on vantait la bonne humeur, semble triste à crever : ce n'est pas vous, vaillants humoristes, qui lui rendrez la joie avec vos petits croquetons, si amusants qu'ils soient.

91

[14] Rouault. Wood-engraved illustration. *Cirque de l'Étoile Filante.* 1938.

that trend. Vollard was an art dealer, and, as a publisher, may be considered more impresario than editor. His artists make an extraordinary list, including Bonnard, Dufy, Picasso, Rouault, and Dunoyer de Segonzac. His first book, Verlaine's *Parallèlement*, was illustrated with large marginal lithographs by Bonnard against which the poetry was set in a generous size of Garamond italic, printed letterpress by the Imprimerie Nationale. After the work was completed in 1900, the directorate of the Imprimerie took exception to the text and recalled the edition, save for a few copies that had been distributed. Vollard's exacting and detailed attention to his books often dragged out their completion for years. At his death in 1939, a score of books were in production and in some instances a quarter of a century had elapsed between commissioning and completion.

[15] Manet. Lithographic Illustration. *The Raven.*

Using painters as illustrators was certainly not a new idea. Édouard Manet and Henri de Toulouse-Lautrec had both led the way in reviving drawing on stone for books. Manet's illustrations for Poe's *Raven* point up the misfortune that he did so few. Not all publishers were as demanding of craftsmen and materials as Vollard in producing *livres de peintres* to meet an ever-growing demand for limited editions. In 1967, Henry Jonquières, an eminent French printer-publisher for the last several decades, told me that the present buyers of deluxe limited editions were increasingly concerned with the value of illustrated books as investments rather than as works of art and were moved more by the name of the artist than by the quality of his prints and the typography that accompanies them.

The Twenties: The Offenbacher Werkstatt

Among the European *ateliers* that began and flourished after World War I, Rudolf Koch's Offenbacher Werkstatt was one of the most professional and influential. It had the character of a private studio, yet it enjoyed the closest possible relationship with an outstanding type foundry and with an excellent arts and crafts school. As instructor of calligraphy at the school, Koch gave some of Germany's finest printers their knowledge of the forms and arrangement of letters. In addition to these personal connections, he had earned the respect and admiration of most of the graphic artists of Europe and of some in the United States, where his types Koch *Antiqua (Eve)* and *Neuland* were introduced in the 1920's.

The Werkstatt consisted of the studio where Koch and his chief assistants worked on the projects that were graphic in nature, and a second large workroom devoted to the making of tapestries, both woven and embroidered. In a nearby building, Gustav Eichenauer maintained a shop for engraving and punch-cutting. Former associates, in other towns, were available for special assignments in mural painting, silversmithing, and calligraphy. The projects undertaken by the Werkstatt were divided between those initiated in the studio, chiefly by Koch, and those which came in as commissions from private, publishing, and ecclesiastical sources. The example of Morris was obvious here, but the manner in which ideas were carried out was much closer to the functioning of a Renaissance than of a Victorian studio.

When I was with the group, in 1931 and 1932, Koch's chief assistant and co-worker was the woodcutter Fritz Kredel. His principal aid in calligraphy was Berthold Wolpe. A third regular helper was Richard Bender, whose job it was to clean up drawings for reproduction and, in some instances, to sharpen the etched lines of finished plates with a graver.

The master of the studio, Koch, was not an administrator. He guided his assistants, all of whom had been his pupils, by a subtle force of personality. He was not a strong man, either in

ÄBCDEFGHIJKLMN
ÖPQRSTÜVWYXZ
äbcdefghijklmnöpqrst
uvwxyzßȝ$&.,:;!?"'=([«-*
†§ȼ1234567890**1234567890**

[16] Eichenauer. Proof of roman type designed by Warren
Chappell and cut in lead by Gustav Eichenauer. 1955.
It was never cast because of the closing of the foundry.

fact or appearance. Born in Nuremberg in 1876, the son of a
sculptor, he was a student at the Munich Academy when his
father's death forced him to seek a trade. Koch chose to become
a goldsmith, and, like Gutenberg, he eventually put some of
that training and experience into cutting type. The three types
which Koch designed directly on metal were his *Jessen, Neuland*, and *Marathon*.

No project undertaken in the Werkstatt better describes
the Koch approach than the making of *Das Blumenbuch*, the
famous book of 250 wild flowers which Koch drew and Fritz
Kredel cut on pearwood. Several years were required to execute the cuts. After that, the printing was done by Kleuken's
Mainzer Press, and the book hand-colored by Emile Woellner,
in Leipzig. It was completed in October of 1930. It was
financed from the beginning by Koch, and was a fully realized
production when it was turned over to the Insel Verlag for
distribution.

The Twenties: Type Design

For printing, World War I was more than an interruption;

it marked the end of an era. At war's end, those who had learned their craft under the influence of the Morris revival and had rediscovered calligraphy through the teaching of Johnston became leaders in the printing arts, and in a number of cases became teachers themselves. Eric Gill, Walter Tiemann, Rudolf Koch, E. R. Weiss, Paul Renner, and Ernst Schneidler were outstanding examples. In the 1920's among the type designers who came into prominence was Jan van Krimpen, chief designer for the Enschedé foundry. His first type, *Lutetia*, was cut and cast in 1924–5 and imported into America shortly afterward. An early use of it is shown in the page from *Jésus Christ en Flandre* privately printed in New York at the Strawberry Hill Press in 1928, with wood engravings by Allen Lewis.

the hour of prayer, at the fall of day, at the moment when nature is silent and the bells speak. The sea cast up a faint, white glimmer, but changing like the color of steel; the sky was mostly gray; in the west long, narrow spaces looked like waves of blood, whereas in the east glittering lines, marked as by a fine pencil, were separated from one another by clouds, folded like the wrinkles on an old man's forehead. Thus the sea and the sky formed a neutral background, everything in half tints, which made the fires of the setting sun glare ominously. The face of nature inspired a feeling of terror. If it is allowable to interweave the daring hyperboles of the people into the written language, one might repeat what the soldier said, "Time is rolling away," or what the peasant answered, that the sky had the look of a hangman. All of a sudden the wind rose in the west, and the skipper, who never ceased to watch the sea, seeing it swell toward the horizon, cried, "Ho, ho!" At this cry the sailors stopped immediately, and let their oars float. ✧ "The skipper's right," said Thomas. The boat, borne on the top of a huge wave, seemed to be descending to the bottom of the gaping sea.

[17] Van Krimpen. *Lutetia* type. *Jésus Christ en Flandre*. 1928.

In late 1957, the year before his death, Van Krimpen and I exchanged views on punch-cutting. He wrote that his own engraver, Helmuth Raedisch, with whom he had worked for 30 years, "has grown, alas, more and more polished." I regretted that our postal colloquy could not have continued, for it seemed to me he must have recognized that his own tight style of working allowed little opportunity for a punch-cutter to make his particular contribution. Van Krimpen quoted Gill: "Letters are things, not pictures of things," and it is exactly that distinction that has been sorely tried today, time and time again.

Koch had an almost equally long association with his punch-cutter, Eichenauer. When I was studying with Koch

auf, legte seinen Mantel um, nahm das Licht, entfernte sich ohne ein Wort zu sagen und kehrte so schnell als möglich in sein Bett zurück. Er konnte dasselbe noch kaum erreicht haben, als der König sich erhob und in das Zimmer der Königin ging, worüber sich diese sehr wunderte. Als er in das Bett gestiegen

und sie freundlich begrüßt hatte, faßte sie sich bei seiner Fröhlichkeit ein Herz und sagte: «O mein Herr, welch neues

[18] Koch. *Wallau* type. Boccaccio's *König Argilulf*. 1932.

and could watch his method of working, I was always aware that his attitude toward the process of designing was creative rather than eclectic. His version of a *rotunda*, called *Wallau*, is shown in a page from a Boccaccio story, printed in 1931–2, with woodcut decorations by Fritz Kredel. Here Koch's *Wallau* and Morris's *Troy*, cut by Prince, are compared:

else in the world, no wonders, no terrors, no unspeakable beauties. Yet when we think what a small part of the world's history, past, present, &

[19] Morris and Koch. Comparison of round gothics, *Troy* above and *Wallau* below.

Als er aber den größten Teil derselben auf die nämliche Weise an einem Punkte geschoren sah, wunderte er sich und sprach bei sich selbst: «Derjenige, den ich

It seems to me that the calligraphic forms of the *Troy* font fail to achieve the naturally organic characteristics of a *rotunda*, instead only imitating the models on which they were based.

In addition to Eichenauer, who worked for the Klingspor foundry, there were other able punch-cutters during the nineteen twenties and early thirties. Louis Hoell, who was associated with the Bauer foundry in Frankfurt, was responsible for the cutting of types designed by Weiss. He also cut special fonts for Dr. Willy Wiegand of the Bremer Press, and for Joseph Blumenthal of the Spiral Press. August Rosenberger, typecutter for D. Stempel, also in Frankfurt, is responsible for the engravings in lead of Hermann Zapf's calligraphic alphabets and exercises published in 1950 under the title *Mit Feder und Stichel*. Working independently, Charles Malin of Paris cut for Gill the first sizes of his *Perpetua*. Malin also worked for Stanley Morison, Frederic Warde, and Giovanni Mardersteig.

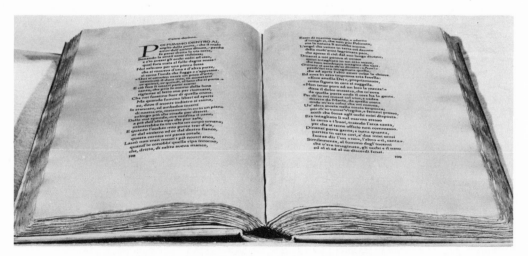

[20] Wiegand. Bremer Press. *Divina Commedia*. 1921.

The Twenties: The Bauhaus

During the 1920's the Bauhaus exerted its greatest influence on typography. Founded in 1919 in Weimar for the integral teaching of art and craft, the Bauhaus included on its original staff Walter Gropius, Marcel Breuer, Vasili Kandinski, Paul Klee, Lyonel Feininger, Joseph Albers, László Moholy-Nagy, and Mies van der Rohe. The Bauhaus ideal, as stated by Gropius, was "a restriction to typical basic form and color, intelligible to all." In type this was expressed by a rationally constructed alphabet, free of serifs and contrasts. Paul Renner was the designer of such a face in 1925. It was cut by the Bauer Type Foundry and named *Futura*. Time has shown it to be the most successful of the sans serif types, and it has long been available for machine composition. Its use, however, has been chiefly for display and advertising. *Futura* and other sans serif types do not have the legibility of the good workaday romans that resulted from printing experience rather than from rationalization. Thus the functionalism preached by the Bauhaus failed where it should have been most effective.

The Twenties: Small Printing Plants

Some of the finest typography and printing of this cen-

COMETH JESUS WITH
THEM UNTO A PLACE
CALLED GETHSEMANE, AND
SAITH UNTO THE DISCIPLES, SIT YE HERE, WHILE I
GO AND PRAY YONDER. AND HE TOOK WITH HIM
Peter and the two sons of Zebedee, and began to be sorrowful and very heavy. Then saith he unto them, My soul is
exceeding sorrowful, even unto death: tarry ye here, and
watch with me. And he went a little farther, and fell on his
face, and prayed, saying, O my Father, if it be possible, let
this cup pass from me: nevertheless not as I will, but as thou
wilt. And he cometh unto the disciples, and findeth them
asleep, and saith unto Peter, What, could ye not watch with
me one hour? Watch & pray, that ye enter not into temptation: the spirit indeed is willing, but the flesh is weak. He
went away again the second time, and prayed, saying, O my
69

[21] Gill. Golden Cockerel Press. *The Four Gospels.* 1931.

tury has come from the specimen printing departments of the
type foundries. Bauer, Klingspor, Stempel, and Enschedé come
first to mind. From time to time a university press has also
produced exceptional work. The Yale University Press, under
the direction of Carl P. Rollins, a most excellent printer whose
connection with the Yale press began in 1916, is an example.
Another press with small facilities that issued some of the note-
worthy printing examples of the twenties was Dr. Wiegand's
Bremer Press. The decoration for his publications was in the
form of initials designed by Anna Simons. Other presses of the
period that were dedicated to fine printing were The Golden
Cockerel and St. Dominic's in England, The Grabhorn Press
and The Pynson Printers in the United States, and the Officina
Bodoni in Italy. The last has been owned and operated since
1922 by Dr. Mardersteig.

The United States: Trade Books and Special Editions

Despite a wide response to the typographic revival, most printing during the early part of this century became more commonplace rather than more conscientious. The development of photomechanical reproduction for color as well as for black-and-white encouraged a school of illustrators that lacked any natural sympathy or understanding for printing as a medium. Nowhere was this more obvious than in the trade books of American publishers. There were some exceptions, and Alfred Knopf, who organized his own firm in 1915, was one. He was sufficiently concerned to seek the help of designers, and he turned to Bruce Rogers and Elmer Adler, who introduced him to others. As a result he managed to achieve a style that has been recognized and has served the house like a trademark. Of those who worked with him, the chief architect of the Knopf typographic style was William Addison Dwiggins (1880–1956), who brought to the task intelligence and taste as well as real talent as a letterer. He worked, at one time or another, with both the Harvard and Yale University Presses. In a long association with the Mergenthaler Linotype Corporation, Dwiggins designed several type faces, including the extensively used *Electra* and *Caledonia*.

America's Vollard was George Macy, whose Limited Editions Club, although founded on the very eve of the depression, was able to survive and flourish. Unlike Vollard, Macy published on a schedule, issuing twelve books a year, in editions of 1,500 copies that were sold by annual subscription. Macy was a man of sensitive literary taste. He was an alumnus of Columbia, the college of Knopf, Bennett Cerf, and many other important figures in American publishing. His choice of artists was catholic, and the range of printers was wide. For both artists and printers the Limited Editions Club's commissions provided an opportunity to make books that the economics of production was making increasingly difficult to manage. As an example of a Macy edition I have chosen *Sister Carrie*. It is a highly personal choice, made on the basis of admiration for the illustrator (Reg-

[22] Limited Editions Club. *Sister Carrie*, printed by Joseph Blumenthal with illustrations by Reginald Marsh.

inald Marsh), the printer (Joseph Blumenthal), and the type face (Janson).

Offset Lithography

The pace of mechanical improvements did not slow with the coming of a new century. In 1904 an offset press was invented for planographic printing on paper. The offset principle had been used for printing from stone onto tin, but the press that a New York lithographer, Ira Rubel, introduced was made possible by the development of metal plates. These could be wrapped around a cylinder and used to run against and print onto a second, rubber-covered cylinder. From this rubber impression the image was transferred to paper. By the end of the

A Short History of the Printed Word

twenties there had been improvement in the quality of offset, and this was even more apparent during the decade of the depression. However, the medium never produced as good results in American as in European hands during its period of development.

Photocomposing Machines

The use of intaglio and planographic impressions eliminates the need for type composition going through a relief stage as cast metal, since both methods utilize photography. The first photocomposing machine was built in England in the early nineteen twenties. Since then, a number of methods have been perfected and put into operation, some of them by the major typesetting manufacturers. They did not come into general use, however, until after World War II.

If there has ever been a single point of agreement among printers, it is that forms and weights of letters should be adjusted to the sizes in which they are used. Thus, in the period before mechanical reproduction of punches and mats, each size was considered independently. That practice was greatly compromised by the employment of pantographic engraving machines, which use large-pattern drawings to produce mechanically reduced punches or mats. With photocomposing, where a single alphabet on film is substituted for various sizes of matrices, the letters can be not only enlarged and reduced, but expanded or condensed, darkened or lightened. Gill's observation is violently turned about to read: letters are *pictures of things,* not things.

In his 1960 Reith lectures, Professor Edgar Wind, an outstanding philosopher and art historian at Oxford, pointed out how "our vision of art has been transformed by reproduction."

Our eyes have been sharpened to those aspects of painting and sculpture that are brought out effectively by a camera. What is more decisive, in the artist's own vision we can observe the growth of a pictorial and sculptural imagination that is posi-

*tively attuned to photography, producing works photogenic to
such a degree that they seem to find a vicarious fulfillment in
mechanized after-images, as if the ultimate hope of a painter or
sculptor today, apart from having his works placed in a museum, would be to see them diffused in comprehensive picture-
books, preferably in an illustrated* catalogue raisonné. *What has
optimistically been called the "museum without walls" is in fact
a museum on paper—a paper-world of art in which the epic
oratory of Malraux proclaims, with the voice of a crier in the
marketplace, that all art is composed in a single key, that huge
monuments and small coins have the same plastic eloquence if
transferred to the scale of the printed page, that a* gouache *can
equal a fresco.*

The Decade Before World War II

The eventual esthetic price of increasing mechanization in
the printing industry was hardly noticeable during the 1930's.
Not only was the world caught up in a crippling depression,
but fascism and communism were creating an atmosphere of
physical threats to match the economic ones. Yet, in the United
States especially, there has never been another time when more
constructive effort was dedicated by individuals and organiza-
tions to improving the appearance and quality of books. The
ranks of our native printers, typographers and graphic artists
were augmented by a number of Europeans, mostly Germans,
who fled the Continent. Koch's two principal co-workers, with
whom I was associated at the Offenbacher Werkstatt, were
among those who left Germany. Berthold Wolpe went to England, where he has taught calligraphy and typography at Johnston's old school, the Royal College of Art. Fritz Kredel came
to America in 1938 and has continued his woodcutting and
illustrating career in New York. Hans Alexander Mueller and
Hugo Steiner-Prag came from the Leipzig Academy, where
they had long been professors. Steiner-Prag's student, Fritz
Eichenberg, became the first director of the graphic arts school
at Pratt Institute. George Salter, a Berlin book designer, was

responsible for a remarkably successful class in calligraphy at Cooper Union that proved to be the training ground for a number of the post–World War II leaders of American typography and lettering. At the time of the invasion of Poland, the books of Vollard, Macy, and Sir Francis Meynell (Nonesuch Press) were representative of the fertility of printing and printmaking during the thirties.

Newspapers in the Twentieth Century

Alfred Harmsworth, who became Lord Northcliffe, was one of England's truly original and powerful newspaper publishers. His *Evening News* and *Daily Mail* were among the most successful of the mass-directed English papers at the end of the nineteenth century. Just at the beginning of the twentieth, Harmsworth met Joseph Pulitzer during an ocean voyage, and out of their conversations came a proposal that Harmsworth be responsible for a single edition of Pulitzer's *New York World*. The result appeared on January 1, 1901—a half-sized newspaper of thirty-two pages. The *World* returned to its customary format after that one issue, but Harmsworth followed up his American experiment with a tabloid of his own, the *London Daily Mirror*, in 1903.

During World War I, while the publishers of the *Chicago Tribune* were both serving in France, one of them, Captain Joseph M. Patterson, met Lord Northcliffe. The captain was advised by Lord Northcliffe to start a tabloid paper in America. Patterson agreed, and with his cousin, Colonel Robert R. McCormick, launched the *Illustrated Daily News* in New York on June 26, 1919. Its success tempted a number of other publishers to produce papers of small size, and by 1940 almost fifty were in circulation. There was more to the concept than merely cutting the size of an eight-column journal in half. The real changes were an increased use of pictures and a reporting style that was concise and lively.

Time, begun in 1923, and *Life*, in 1936, represented a similar concept of news coverage. The former influenced the departmentalized journalism of the thirties, while its sister publication established new standards for the gathering and printing of picture-reporting. Like the newspapers, the news magazines have hastened a number of mechanical developments in type composition, plate-making and presswork.

In the fall of 1915, *The New York Times* started its *Mid-Week Pictorial*, a supplement in tabloid size, which provided outstanding picture coverage during the remaining years of World War I. I recall it as being a cross between the continental illustrated news magazines of that time, and the future picture magazine *Life*. As early as 1913, the *Times* had bought rotogravure presses, and had begun experimenting with them. In April of 1914, it began printing Sunday supplements. By 1930, eighty newspapers had rotogravure sections, but some of these were eliminated during the depression of the ensuing decade. Most revealing is the fact that of the sixty-five which remained in 1940, only ten were printed on equipment owned independently by their publishers.

The problem of independent ownership of the means of production has affected the nature of publishing to an ever-increasing degree. The difficulties of operating the equipment can be staggering even for those who can afford ownership. The steady pressure toward consolidation that has created surviving newspaper empires is just as indicative of the rising costs in plant and operation as it is witness to the aggressiveness of owners.

Stanley Morison, one of the century's most influential typographic scholars, served for years as adviser on format and type for *The Times* of London. Despite his great knowledge and sensitivity, the nature of newspaper publication restricted the scope of his contributions. Subtle typography and elegant presswork cannot be expected of the daily press. The chief contribution of newspapers to the graphic arts industry has been in spurring the development of some of the major tools of production. In this connection, three dates stand out: 1814, when power was first applied to the press, 1865, when rotary printing from curved plates was perfected, and 1890, when the

Linotype machine was put into production. Each of these events changed some aspect of the nature of printing. Newspapers were metamorphosed from four- and eight-page publications issued casually when there was sufficient news to warrant a printing, into multi-paged editions which were on-and-off the press and into the streets daily. Only a hundred and fifty years ago, the majority of newspapers and books were printed on presses that required the forms to be run in and out under the platen just as in Gutenberg's time, and pressure was hand-applied through a lever.

CHAPTER X

The Twentieth Century: After 1940

IN 1940, THE COLLAPSE of France obscured any general cele-
bration of the 500th anniversary of Gutenberg's invention
of movable type. However, a number of books were made that
year to mark the occasion. None was more impressive than the
unique *Aventur und Kunst* by Konrad Bauer. The book was
printed at the Bauer Type Foundry in Frankfurt. Konrad
Bauer, who was, by the way, not related to the founder of the
Bauersche Giesserei, was one of the most original of contemporary scholars in paleography and typographic history. His
achievement, in *Aventur und Kunst,* was the searching out,
arranging and illustrating of five hundred entries, one for each
year from 1440 to 1940, which covered events, personalities, inventions, and publications highlighting the history of printing.

The vigor of European bookmaking was revealed by the
Vollard editions exhibited in the French Pavilion at the New
York World's Fair in 1939. And in the same year, in America,
George Macy began issuing his Limited Editions Club Shake-
speare, in thirty-seven volumes designed by Bruce Rogers.
Each volume was illustrated by a different artist.

By the end of the half millennium of printing, a number of
notable changes were taking place in the average printing shop.
Hand composition was becoming increasingly rare, except for
use in titling and advertising. The cutting of steel punches had
been virtually abandoned. Those types that were being cut by
hand were engraved in lead, in a size twice as large as the letters
on this page. The great majority of types were being produced
by pantographic engraving machines from large pattern drawings. In less than fifty years, machine composition had become
the rule, and by 1940, Linotype dominated that field.

In a very subtle way, the economics of production divorced the compositor and the pressman, and the average printer became reconciled to buying his composition from specialty houses. This meant that he ordered his type like yardgoods, and no longer had the opportunity for immediate adjustments to the type in the composing stick that is part of hand composition.

World War II: 1939–1945

The war acted as a brake on the forward movement of technical developments. After Pearl Harbor, American printers began to feel the pinch of paper rationing and other restrictions that affected the supply and quality of most materials during that period. On the other hand, the demand for books was great, and it was a rare publisher who did not read the signs as pointing to an ever-increasing market for his products. Seeds of change were being planted, however, in the 1939–45 period, and they were to affect the publishers' optimism in ways then unimaginable.

The technological revolution that began in the early 1940's, and is still in progress, did not make itself felt in the general area of communications for a number of years after the war. Replacement of plants and equipment that had been destroyed, or had simply worn out, had to come first. The pressure, and financing, of war research brought about the rapid development of the sophisticated machinery that has come to dominate printing in the 1960's. The Industrial Revolution that shaped the nineteenth century was brought about chiefly by the application of power to tools. In the second half of the twentieth century, it is the application of the swift advances in electronics that have touched almost every industry, profession, trade, and all means of communication.

During the war, television and computers were mere promises for the future. It was the immediate demand for books which chiefly influenced production. Restrictions on materials and equipment were naturally greater in England and France than in the United States; nevertheless the appetite for books was described as *ravenous* in all three countries. In France, some publishers and printers who had reserves of good paper continued to maintain high standards in their books. Picasso's illustrated edition of *Histoire Naturelle*, published in Paris in

[1] Picasso. Aquatint illustration for Buffon's *Histoire Naturelle*. 1942.

1942 by Fabiani, is an example. His sugar aquatints for the famous Buffon text are outstanding examples of the artist's appreciation of the technical resources of intaglio. In 1944, the same publisher, Fabiani, issued *Pasiphaé*, by de Montherlant, with engravings by Matisse. Such special editions provided a sharp contrast in quality to those publications classified as trade editions. In France, as in England, choice of materials came to an end with rationing, and both publisher and purchaser learned to accept what was available. In the English *Economy Agreement,* publishers were governed by a set of self-imposed rules which established size of type and area relationship to the page. Added to this, the constant attrition of plant equipment and a shortage of labor made the printers' and publishers' task even more difficult. Paper rationing did not end in England until 1949.

During the German occupation of Holland, S. L. Hartz, an artist whose principal work was engraving postage stamps for the Haarlem firm of Enschedé, was forced to go underground. He used that period to make a study of type design and the result was a set of punches for a roman font, in 12-point size, which he completed just as the war ended. It was christened *Emergo.* Hartz is one of the few remaining artists who can cut his own designs. He became the successor to Van Krimpen, at Enschedé, after the latter's death.

One of the results of the huge demand for books during the war was the publication of a large number of illustrated classics. This was partly a result of the success enjoyed by the special editions published by Macy's Limited Editions Club and Heritage Club, and Peter Beilenson's Peter Pauper Press. In addition, wartime price controls protected manufacturing costs, and excess-profit taxes encouraged more liberal expenditures on design and plates.

The demand for illustrators and typographers that was created by these projects helped to increase the number of prospective students for classes in the graphic arts. In turn, this demand gave rise to departments devoted to calligraphy, typography, typesetting, hand-press printing, and printmaking. Such departments were set up at many established institutions. The federal law providing financial help to ex-servicemen for training in fields of their choice was an added stimulus to teaching programs.

The enthusiasm of the period was caught up and carried forward in classes like those initiated by George Salter at

Cooper Union, Ray Nash at Dartmouth, and Leonard Baskin at Smith College. And as a dividend of such exposure to what Updike called the "broad and humanizing" work of typography, the ranks of private press owners increased.

The Postwar Years: Type

The need of the printing industry to restock and rebuild had made little progress in England as late as 1950. In the United States, some research had been maintained by most manufacturers of type during the war, but there were no major developments that had left the drawing boards and begun to influence the nature of printing. One firm, the American Type Founders, which had been put together through a long series of corporate amalgamations of type foundries and printing machinery manufacturers, ended the war looking for another field in which to invest. In several moves, the company divested itself of its printing interests, in favor of electronics. It is indicative of the diminished demand for hand-set type, that the foundry division of American Type Founders became a stepchild, and ceased to have any influence on postwar typography.

Perhaps the most striking recovery was that of D. Stempel, the Frankfurt foundry which has cut Linotype matrices for many years as well as produced faces for hand composition. Stempel was helped in its recovery by its relationship to the Mergenthaler Linotype Company. However, the success of its foundry type program is due in large part to Hermann Zapf, an outstanding calligrapher and letterer who has produced some of the most popular type faces of the past two decades. He was not a pupil of Rudolf Koch, but did work for a short time with Koch's son, Paul, a punch-cutter and hand-press printer, and he also taught in Offenbach, in what had once been Koch's class in calligraphy.

In 1967, Stempel completed a Garamond-like type face called *Sabon*, which was designed by Jan Tschichold, a former teacher at the Leipzig Academy now living in Switzerland. *Sabon* may well be one of the last major efforts to produce a

ABCDEFGHIJKLMNOPQ
RSTUVWXYZÄÖÜ
abcdefghijklmnopqrstuvwxyz
ßchckfffififlft&äöü
1234567890 1234567890
.,:;-!?.'()[]*†‹›»«„"/£$

[2] Tschichold. *Sabon* roman.

letterpress face on a grand scale, and thus represents the culmi-
nation of five hundred years of attempts—starting with Nicolas
Jenson—to cut and cast a Roman-inspired type face for relief
printing. Its design is in no way original; it is completely eclectic. It represents, however, an extremely practical collaboration
of basic type-producing systems and this gives it unusual flexibility in shop use. *Sabon* has been cut concurrently for hand
composition and Linotype, by Stempel, and for Monotype by
the English Monotype Corporation, in identical, interchangea-
ble forms. Its forms echo those of the flowering of roman type
in the hands of Claude Garamond. They also represent the
experience of a contemporary designer who has had almost
fifty years to think about them in terms of twentieth-century
methods and usage.

Despite such credentials, *Sabon* was not immediately purchased by the composition houses of Europe and the United
States. In part, this is due to the rapid changes taking place in
the very nature of printing. There is, in fact, some question
whether the concept of *impression*, as it has been discussed in
these pages, is not in danger of giving way to methods of
duplication that will dispense entirely with the use of ink. In

the realm of typesetting, photocomposition is rapidly replacing the use of hot metal, and it is only reasonable to assume that the press could give way to some method related to photoprinting or even to the popular dry copiers.

In addition to Tschichold and Zapf, several others stand out among those contributing to contemporary type designing: Hartz of Holland, Reynolds Stone of England, Giovanni Mardersteig of Italy, Georg Trump of Germany, and Max Caflisch and Walter Schneider of Switzerland. Schneider, like Hartz, is a punch-cutter as well as artist. Stone has long been known for his notable work as a wood engraver. Those who knew the work of John Howard Benson, the letterer and stone-cutter, must always regret that he was never drawn into the field of type designing. From his student days at the Art Students' League, where he worked with Joseph Pennell and Allen Lewis, Benson constantly revealed himself as one of the ablest graphic artists of his time. In addition to his contributions to letter forms cut in stone, he completed two books, *The Elements of Lettering*, with A. G. Carey, and a calligraphic translation of Ludovico Arrighi's *First Writing Book*.

The Postwar Years: Printing

Because the design and manufacture of new machinery was retarded by the war, small, individually owned shops were little changed, during the latter years of the 1940's, from their physical appearance and operating style of the preceding decade. In recalling the names of Blumenthal's Spiral Press, Beilenson's Walpole Printing Office, and Fred Anthoensen's Southworth Anthoensen Press, as examples, one is struck by the fact that such shops are usually projections of the personalities who operate them. Perhaps no printing office of this century has survived so long, or kept its commitment to fine printing as consistently as Mardersteig's Officina Bodoni. This press was founded at Montagnola di Lugano, Italy, in 1923, and was moved to Verona in 1927. Another press with the highest standards of commercial printing was The Curwen Press, di-

236

rected by Oliver Simon. Simon was responsible for the printing of *The Fleuron* and *Signature,* two excellent publications devoted to typography.

The specimen-printing department of D. Stempel is not comparable to the usual small commercial establishments, except for the nature of its equipment. It was able, however, to fulfill a similar function with its Trajanus-Presse, and, under the typographic direction of Gotthard de Beauclair, published a series of books. Among these was Aristophanes' *Die Frösche,* illustrated with wood engravings by Imre Reiner. The blocks are engraved in a style that carries on a tradition going back at

Euripides

Laß erst mich doch zu Ende sagen den ganzen Vers!

›Oineus in der Scheune sammelnd der Ernte reiche Frucht,

Erstlinge opfernd‹ —

Aischylos   Stimmt die alte Leier an!

Dionysos

Inmitten des Opfers? pfiff·man ihm auch das alte Lied?

Euripides

Freund, laß ihn nur; versuchen soll ers mal mit dem:

›Zeus, wie es die Wahrheit selber uns berichtet hat‹ —

Dionysos

Du verlierst! denn er sagt gleich

›Stimmt die alte Leier an!‹

Wie eine Feigenwarze sitzt am Augenlid,

107

[3] De Beauclair. Trajanus Presse. Aristophanes' *Die Frösche,* with wood engravings by Imre Reiner.

[4] Daumier. Detail, wood engraving in *Le Monde Illustré*.
1869.
[5] Rouault. Detail, wood engraving, for *Cirque de l'Étoile
Filante*. 1939.
[6] Reiner. Detail, wood engraving, for *Die Frösche*.

least a century; Reiner, who studied with the famous German
calligrapher Ernst Schneidler, is himself responsible for several
type faces. He is a good example of the artist who is so familiar
with the work of the past that he does not have to reinvent or
imitate it. Details from three engravings are shown: Daumier
engraved by Étienne (1869), Rouault engraved by Aubert
(1939), and Reiner engraved by himself (1945).

The specimen printery at Klingspor, in Offenbach, did not
survive the war by many years. This foundry was unable to
recoup its great losses in mats and machinery, and still compete
with the changed market for handset type. The Klingspor shop
was one of the most perfect I have ever seen. Under the guid-
ance of Ernst Engel and Max Dorn, it was the training ground
for some of Europe's foremost typographers and printers.

By 1950, rising costs and the prospect of bigger and faster
presses had made plain the basic problems that small independent printers could expect to face in future competition. Such

economic factors, and the nature of the designer-training programs just before, during, and after the war, led to an increase in the number of studio-oriented typographers, at the expense of shop-trained ones. Some of them have been instinctive printers, but the average one is more of an arranger than a designer. This distinction between the talented and the adequate has always existed. But today, with modern methods tending to increase the gap separating design and execution, control over the medium becomes less subtle and the demands on a typographer are correspondingly greater.

One heartening influence, presently at work, could act to maintain a healthy respect for good letter forms, and that is the continuing interest in calligraphy. There may be more people in the world today who can recognize good roman and italic alphabets than at any time in the past few centuries. Remembering that it was the presence of great calligraphy which accounted for seminal expressions in type design, it is reasonable to hope that something comparable could happen in our own time. On the other hand, it is discouraging that in the last years of the 1960's there have been designers who were sufficiently exposed to the calligraphic reformation to be aware of history, yet chose to rejuvenate the corpse of *art nouveau*. This reminds me of a story I heard Emil Rudolf Weiss tell of his early years as a painter, when he was producing large canvases filled with classically inspired figures swathed in flowing draperies. One day he was visited by his aging former teacher, Hans Thoma. After studying the work Weiss had in progress on the easel, Thoma commented: "I did something very much like that when I was your age, and *it* wasn't any good either."

The Technological Revolution

A review of printing equipment in 1950 could be summed up in this general way: the new machines for letterpress stressed higher speeds and multicolor printing. Offset lithography, which had improved steadily over the preceding twenty years, showed advances in web presses capable of producing multicolor printing of acceptable quality from continuous rolls of paper. The introduction of bi-metallic plates promised greatly increased durability. In the field of gravure, there were advances in the means of controlling register and color. There were no radical changes in conventional typesetting machines, but those for photocomposition became a practical reality. One such substitution of camera for casting mechanisms was past the testing stage and was available to the trade. Others were in the process of being perfected and produced.

None of these advances was startling. The new press equipment did help to improve the cost factor and general appearance of paperback books, which had finally taken hold in the United States through the use of an expanded system of distribution akin to that of newspapers and magazines. The real revolution in printing is being brought about through the application of electronic technology, directly, through computerized automation, and indirectly, through the influence of television. The effect of the latter on reading habits has been too obvious to require comment. That the effect has been sufficiently fundamental to have outlasted the novelty of the new medium is the important fact. Television networks may hire newspaper reporters and depend in part on news-service tickers for their raw material, but the press is under much greater pressure from the airwaves than conversely.

The use of computers in setting type, as in other applications, is remarkable. A relatively large area of the human judgments called upon for type composition can be handled at inhuman speeds by an electronic brain, removing the drudgery that is associated with any repetitive process. Certain judgments, however, can not be made by mechanical means. These are the ones that can lift a piece of printing above the merely adequate. The most experienced typographer is presented with a new basis for judgment when he sees a first type proof of his original design. Even so experienced a designer as Rogers was notorious for the succession of corrections he demanded in order to achieve pages which would satisfy his taste. Naturally, a skilled compositor provides a typographer with the fewest surprises, because he is able to understand the spirit as well as the specifications of the typographic plan presented to him. The most sophisticated electronic device cannot provide the kind of sensitive response that should be the mark of a good journeyman typesetter. It is possible to envisage the future compositor as a glorified typist.

The Purpose of Printing

The wartime vision of unlimited demand for all kinds of books was greatly altered by the advent of instant news and entertainment through television. Concurrently, the rising cost of printing took its toll in the quality of hardbound books, and in the practicability of publishing small editions. Rising costs also helped to doom many of the magazines and newspapers that had dominated the publishing scene during the first half of the century.

It is possible that books as repositories of human experience and creativeness may be overshadowed, or in time replaced, by microfilm, because of the requirements of space or research. But for an author, there can be no substitute for a well-designed, well-printed, and well-bound edition of his manuscript, that he can hold in his hands to see and feel as well as read. When the purpose of printing is to produce cheap, disposable copies, as is the case with paperbacks, high-speed rotary presses are functional and acceptable. Such means, however, seldom provide the esthetic aspect of reading—the feel and look of a good page that is just as desirable in the twentieth century as it was in the fifteenth.

When Gutenberg set out to make books, his purpose was to compete with the copyists of his time, by cutting the cost of production. His process began by being imitative. However, his design of letters and format mirrored manuscripts at a high point in the history of calligraphy. He was surrounded by an appreciation of the shaping and use of letters. Today, the use of photocomposition and offset printing can be said to produce an imitation of printing, a *picture* of type that is not tactile in either form or impression. The important question is: are the models for such printing comparably as good as those which influenced Gutenberg, when he was imitating manuscripts? Gutenberg's solution to an essentially economic pressure had the added virtue of decreasing the usual percentage of errors normally made by careless or ignorant copyists. The newest and biggest offset presses have the disadvantage of making any corrections more expensive and difficult than before, because of the increased size of the unit which would have to be involved, after final proofs and plate-making.

A basic change that has been brought about by camera techniques is the preparation of whole books as *camera-ready copy*. The pages are pasted into position for photographing, rather than locked into position for electrotyping. Such a procedure can cause the pages to dance and if the camera work is shoddy the image can float. It is known that the invention of printing increased literacy and heightened the appreciation of language. But there is a great question as to whether mere multiplication can bring about comparable results.

In 1930, José Ortega y Gasset wrote that the mass-man took the civilization into which he was born as a matter of course, "as spontaneous and self-producing as Nature." This, claimed Ortega, made a primitive of him, with civilization his forest. It is a timely concept, of man as a consumer rather than as one involved and at the service of the basic cultural values of his time. It is difficult to perceive any great literary sensitivity coming as the result of the flood of print that has turned reading into a process of gulping rather than savoring. Certainly no remarkable renaissance in art has accompanied the publication in ever greater numbers, of bigger and more colorful books on painting. And obviously music is not better understood because it assails the ears on every side and to a degree never before imagined in the history of mankind.

Assimilating Mechanization

If this book has an epigraph, it is Horace's motto: *Littera*

[7] Modern production offset press printing five colors consecutively on both sides of continuous rolls.

scripta manet—"the written word remains." That is what makes writing and its offspring printing such special means of communication. Ideas that are completely expressed in type and impressed on the page represent the considered judgments of the author. In the passage from Milton, "he who destroys a good book kills reason itself, kills the image of God, as it were in the eye," the preciousness of books is summed up. It would be an unhappy exchange if modern means were only able to produce more printing, more rapidly.

Obviously, the constantly evolving technology requires a new sense of dedication on the part of those who use it. Many of the most promising-looking of the new techniques are deceptive. They offer too little resistance and encourage slickness —what Baudelaire described as *chic*, which he compared with "the work of those writing masters who, with an elegant hand and a pen shaped for italic or running script, can shut their eyes and boldly trace the head of Christ or Napoleon's hat in the form of a flourish." Yet the new techniques are here to stay and will certainly find their masters as have all those that came before.

Mere techniques are always apt to degenerate into mannerisms. For this reason photographic type composition requires a greater degree of supervision than the more conventional cast composition for letterpress. Both Fournier and Didot were excellent craftsmen, and extremely intelligent as well, yet because they lacked highly developed models for their alphabets they corrupted letter forms in a way that affected the appearance of a large proportion of nineteenth-century typography.

As far as type is concerned it is helpful to realize that the letters of the alphabet, being symbols and abstract in themselves, are most successful when their forms come closest to being free from idiosyncrasy. With such a realization, type designing becomes a search for the obvious and universal, not for what is branded as original but is really improvisational.

It is equally imperative that the results of applying modern technology to presswork be constantly measured against the most primitive printing, so that the lessons of the importance of impression and stiff ink may continue as standards for the appearance of words on paper. The key to the comparison should rest in the answer to the question: "Does the page look like an original?" A good page of letterpress printing *is* an original. It is not a picture of a page of type, it is not a reduction, it is an impression made from the type itself, or a direct casting from it. In this simple fact lies the integrity of letterpress printing. It is a three-dimensional process, and type-cutting by hand as it was originally practiced was also a three-dimensional process, sculptural in nature. The methods that made possible Gutenberg's first page of printing have not been supplanted in the 1960's as criteria against which to measure the progress of printing.

INDEX

Italicized page numbers indicate the location of illustrations.

Index

Index

Index

Index

Index

A Note About the Author

WARREN CHAPPELL was born in 1904 in Richmond, Virginia. He is a graduate of the University of Richmond, and attended the Art Students League of New York, the Offenbacher Werkstatt, and the Colorado Springs Fine Arts Center. He has written on the graphic arts and is the author of a number of children's books. He is known chiefly as an illustrator, typographer, and type designer, having been responsible for the format and decoration of several hundred books. Mr. Chappell and his wife presently live in Norwalk, Connecticut.

A Note on the Type

This book was set on the Linotype in Janson, a recutting made direct from type cast from matrices long thought to have been made by the Dutchman Anton Janson, who was a practicing type founder in Leipzig during the years 1668–87. However, it has been conclusively demonstrated that these types are actually the work of Nicholas Kis (1650–1702), a Hungarian, who most probably learned his trade from the master Dutch type founder Dirk Voskens. The type is an excellent example of the influential and sturdy Dutch types that prevailed in England up to the time William Caslon developed his own incomparable designs from them.

Typography and binding design by

WARREN CHAPPELL